Praise for *NOTES FRO*

This book is amazing. Andy shows us how God can be ther
This book is unflinchingly honest, rooted in eternal truth, fi

— **Dr. Ray Pritchard**, president, Keep Believing Ministries; author, *Why Did This Happen to Me?*

Andy has a wonderful story to tell—but don't expect to get the cymbals and trumpets out just yet. Let him take you into the dark depths of his pain and sorrow and concerns for his family and church and friends. Take this journey with Andy and your heart will swell with glory for the good work of God in our world today.

— **Scot McKnight**, professor of New Testament, Northern Seminary; author

Andy's foundation and framework is solidly scriptural but also very practical. You'll discover both classic and contemporary illustrations to help broaden any cancer victim's perspective on this dreaded disease. What a gift this book is to those who battle cancer, but also to the body of Christ to help all of us minister to those who are ill.

— **Dr. Gene A. Getz**, professor, pastor, author, Plano, TX

Andy addresses the hard questions everyone asks of God during times of suffering by challenging them to think biblically, while helping them keep an eternal focus. All believers who are suffering in any way will resonate with the deep truths that are skillfully exposed and will find it easy to apply them to their own situations.

— **Mark L. Bailey**, president and professor, Dallas Theological Seminary

The only thing more terrifying than learning that one has cancer is the prospect of going through it alone. No one has to fear that any more. This book can be your companion and guide, pointing you to the hope and the peace that comes from knowing that God walks the pathway with you. Read it slowly. Read it carefully. Read it well.

— **Mark Young**, president, Denver Theological Seminary

In this powerfully revealing book, my friend Andy McQuitty shares his own journey in a way that is at the same time transparent and transformational. If you are battling cancer (or have a loved one who is), you need to read this book. It will encourage you to continue your fight and empower you to strengthen your faith!

— **Ed Young**, pastor; author, *You! The Journey to the Center of Your Worth*

For all its darkness, Cancerland is no God-forsaken place. Those who have walked the Valley with Him find our Lord is more intimately present here than most places on our planet. Andy's writing is warmly personal, biblically insightful, greatly encouraging, and often humorous. The good news is that you don't have to walk this lonesome valley by yourself!

— **Stu Weber**, pastor and author

Andy's friendship has always been a gift to me, but watching him accept his assignment to go through the Valley of cancer taught me much and has inspired me as I deal with my own life disappointments and struggles. Whatever season of life you find yourself in, I know Andy's wisdom and writing will deeply touch you.

— **Ben Crane**, PGA Tour golf professional

This book is raw and rugged, not only about the realities of cancer, but more importantly about the gritty side of ruthless trust in God. If you are fighting what appears to be a losing battle with cancer, I urge you to listen to and heed the insights of this veteran.

— **Bill Hendricks**, author, *The Light That Never Dies: A Story of Hope in the Shadows of Grief*

Perhaps you or someone you know is walking through the Valley and asking the "why me?" question. Andy McQuitty is your Travel Guide through Cancerland. He isn't just a pastor providing comfort and spiritual answers. He is a fellow traveler who has been there and can share his observations and relevant Scripture. Notes from the Valley *provides hope from a personal and biblical perspective.*

— **Kerby Anderson**, president, Probe Ministries; host, *Point of View*

It is so difficult for Christians to be transparent about the real life challenges they face. That is not the case for Andy McQuitty, an author and pastor who invites us into his experience with cancer. Andy serves as a reliable guide to readers for whom the topic of cancer has hit home. Notes from the Valley *is honest and real.*

— **Mark A. Yarhouse**, PsyD, professor of psychology, Regent University

No prepublication of a book have I felt more compelled to forward to friends and Andy McQuitty's fellow-travelers in the deep valley of the gloomy shadow of focused death. However, I shall wait to share its rich presentation of Scripture and theology from the most credible pulpit of a pastor and preacher—his ongoing experience of suffering.

— **Ramesh Richard**, president, RREACH; professor, Dallas Theological Seminary

My wife and I lost our youngest daughter to cancer, and we know that the desert is indeed part of the Valley. We can and must find healing for our broken hearts. May the words written in this book assure you that God's love is stronger than cancer or any valley you face.

— **James Robison**, president, LIFE Outreach International, Cohost, LIFE Today

If you or a loved one is struggling with cancer allow Andy to guide you through the Valley. He lives there, he knows, and he's just a few feet ahead of you on the path.

— **Pete Briscoe,** senior pastor, Bent Tree Bible Fellowship

In the struggle of your life, you need a travel guide who's journeyed the terrain of pain. A cancer survivor, Andy McQuitty has walked through the valley of death while drinking deep from the fountain of life. Notes from the Valley *is the rare book that addresses hard questions with hope and heart. With Andy as your guide, the quest for survival will lead to a bigger discovery—real LIFE.*

— **Allen Arnold**, director of content and resources, Ransomed Heart Ministries

Have you been looking for a book to give a family fighting with cancer? You've found it! Andy's book is very personal, based on his own extended time in this deep, dark valley of cancer. It is the mixture of truth and inspiration he longed for during his many months of struggle. This is a deeply insightful gospel perspective of both life and death.

— **Bobb Biehl**, executive mentor, founder and president, Consulting Institute

Andy McQuitty pulls back the curtain on his journey of rediscovery of the goodness and faithfulness of God. One way that God has redeemed Andy's suffering is the insights that all of us gain from his notes from the valley.

— **Steve Stroope**, author, *Tribal Church,* lead pastor Lake Pointe Church, TX

Andy recounts his honest emotions alongside humorous reflections while traversing the treacherous terrain of colon cancer treatment. If you find yourself in the valley, read this book. With Andy as your guide you will be anchored to divine Truth, and your journey together will be filled with healthy doses of hope and encouragement.

— **John Nieder,** LIVE THE WORD, Dallas, TX

In life, it is important to have a mentor who has experience in things positive and negative, and has the skill to communicate those experiences. I believe it is imperative that a mentor has great command of how to apply the Scriptures to our lives in all circumstances. Andy has all of these qualities mastered, and I hope you will rejoice in the wisdom he shares in these pages.

— **Justin Leonard,** PGA Tour player

Andy McQuitty accepted his "gift from God" so he can minister to so many others who live with this disease. As James 1:2 says, "Consider it pure joy, my brothers and sisters, whenever you face trials of many kinds," Andy shares the joy that he received through God's love during his battle with cancer.

— **Mark Teixeira,** first baseman, New York Yankees

Andy is my friend, and I know that the words on these pages truly reflect the work God has done in his life and his heart through an extremely difficult season. This book is authentic, instructive, and full of hope.

— **Rev. Toby Slough**, senior pastor, Crosstimbers Community Church

NOTES *from the* VALLEY

A SPIRITUAL TRAVELOGUE THROUGH CANCER

ANDY McQUITTY

MOODY PUBLISHERS
CHICAGO

All emphases in Scripture quotations have been placed by the author.

Edited by Pam Pugh
Interior design: Design Corps
Author photo: Hansel Dodds at Hansel Photography
Cover design: Studio Gearbox
Cover image of Death Valley desert scene copyright © 2013 by Thomas Hawk/Stocksy 13834.
All rights reserved.

Library of Congress Cataloging-in-Publication Data

McQuitty, Eric A. (Eric Andrew)
Notes from the valley : a spiritual travelogue through cancer / Eric A. (Andy) McQuitty.
pages cm
Includes bibliographical references.
ISBN 978-0-8024-1254-6
1. Cancer—Patients—Religious life. 2. Suffering—Religious aspects—Christianity. 3. Cancer—Religious aspects—Christianity. 4. Death—Religious aspects—Christianity. 5. McQuitty, Eric A. (Eric Andrew) I. Title.
BV4910.33.M38 2015
248.8'61969940092—dc23
[B]

2014028742

We hope you enjoy this book from Moody Publishers. Our goal is to provide high-quality, thought-provoking books and products that connect truth to your real needs and challenges. For more information on other books and products written and produced from a biblical perspective, go to www.moodypublishers.com or write to:

Moody Publishers
820 N. LaSalle Boulevard
Chicago, IL 60610

3 5 7 9 10 8 6 4 2

Printed in the United States of America

To my beloved Irving Bible Church family
whose love and prayers sustained and encouraged me
every step of the way through the Valley . . .

CONTENTS

FOREWORD: NOTES FROM THE VALLEY

I spent the first seven years of ministry at The Village Church, where I am lead pastor, trying to prepare men and women for the reality of suffering. I watched as many of my friends and co-laborers were crushed on the rocks of sorrow without the strong support of understanding how God is at work in the mess. Cotton candy Christianity left them sick and helpless when meat would have strengthened them for the seas ahead. Without any wisdom or knowledge of God's call to suffering, His provision in suffering, and His promise to always be all that we need, these individuals were unable to say with Charles Spurgeon, "I have learned to kiss the wave that throws me upon the Rock of Ages." Instead, they shattered and sank or fell prey to the ridiculous theologies that make God a genie in a bottle and make us Aladdin.

Teaching on suffering is scarce these days, as most people seem to be drawn more toward teachings on pragmatic topics. These topics are important and should be dealt with biblically and faithfully, but the one thing we all have in common regardless of age, race, education, or socioeconomic status is that we will all suffer. The world is broken; no one will make it through life without experiencing this reality.

To not enter the fray of suffering with the calming, peace-bringing, hope-strengthening Word of God is to leave people to myths and empty hopes. I am grateful that Andy is sharing his story with us and pointing to our loving heavenly Father as he does. I am a traveler alongside him and maybe alongside you. I was diagnosed with primary brain cancer in 2009 and was told that I had two to three years to live. One of God's great mercies to me happened while I was trying to get other people ready: He was graciously getting me ready. As I read the book, it resonated that you are holding my soul, and I felt old emotions and joys.

When Andy writes of "the barren wilderness" and "the valley of the shadow of death," I remember hearing the news. I remember hearing the words *cancer, craniotomy, resection, neuro-rehab.* My soul dropped and for several days, I couldn't find the ground. I had my own "why me, why not them" moment and wrestled with why God would lay this path before me. I wept as I read chapter 2, "Immanuel," because once again I remembered a type of peace that didn't make sense, a deep type of joy that wouldn't leave regardless of how sick the medicine made me or what I was told my chances were. God was with me, and it made all the difference.

It was during this season that I learned that happiness and joy are not one and the same. Joy is much more stable than the fragility of happiness. Dark nights of the soul are better navigated with good guides. Andy is a good guide. If you are personally traveling this path, I believe this book will touch you. It will make you laugh as you start to feel less alone, knowing others have been where you are. We have stood on the precipice, we have wrestled with our fears, we have clung to Jesus, and He has carried us through. I am praying for your strength, faith, and healing.

Your Fellow Traveler,

Matt Chandler

WELCOME: TRAVEL TIPS FOR THE VALLEY

Dear Fellow Travelers,

I am assuming that you are perusing these words because you or someone you love has been tapped by God to go on a trip to the Land of Cancer.[1] If that is true, I'd like to offer you my condolences quickly followed up by a hearty welcome to the journey.

I have received my own posting orders to Cancerland and can attest to the grating, fearful, unbelieving sense of desperation they inevitably bring. I'm so sorry you are having to deal with this most unwelcome invitation to such an unexpected journey with an uncertain destination. You know intuitively that you are in for a tough trip at best, and therefore I won't sugarcoat it as a tourist's jaunt to a vacation spot. It's actually an arduous trip through a desert valley, and I truly wish you could avoid it altogether.

But since you are already a bona fide, card-carrying invitee on this difficult trek, I may as well welcome you. It is not a trip any of us wanted to make, but since we're going, we might as well make the best of it, don't you think? And we really can, you know. The desert may not be Shangri La, but it does have its charms, especially since, as people of faith, our guide is God Himself. As a cancer survivor friend whispered in my ear when he hugged me at the news of my own diagnosis, "This is the most difficult journey you'll ever take but also the most blessed." He was right. Membership in the cancer club may not be the hottest ticket in town, but it is inarguably one of the most exclusive. So welcome aboard, fellow traveler. We Christ-followers who are already in this Valley are so happy to have your company with our motley but hopeful crew.

As a Christian minister, it has been my privilege to travel the world over. Most of those trips have been both strenuous and blessed, just like our joint venture to Cancerland. On each one, I've benefitted greatly from the advice and tips of guides who have gone before me. Whether it was negotiating a coup attempt in Haiti, nocturnally bouncing at high speed around mountain corners in Congo, or picking my way through a sodden Colombian rain forest at nightfall, I relied on the wisdom of trusted travelers who had gone before me to keep me instructed, motivated, and encouraged along the way.

But then I suddenly boarded the express train for the Land of Cancer at 2:58 p.m. on July 14, 2009, with these post-colonoscopy words from my doctor. "Andy, you have a massive tumor that has broken through the wall of your colon. It's cancer. It's serious. Get in here now." Perhaps you have recently heard similar words from your physician. If so, I'm confident that you share my amazement at how completely the cancer diagnosis changes everything. One moment I'm sitting at my desk, minding my own business and tinkering with the possibility of playing golf on Saturday afternoon. The next moment my business had changed from leading a church to battling cancer, and I wound up not playing golf but donating twelve inches of my colon to medical science. That was a triple bogey I frankly had not anticipated. Perhaps you can relate!

However the fun was just beginning as I realized that, though I still physically lived in Texas, what amounted to my death sentence (I was given only an 8 percent chance of surviving Stage IV colon cancer) had instantly transported me to a wholly different spiritual and emotional country that Jeremiah 2:6 (KJV) describes as "the wilderness . . . a land of deserts and of pits, through a land of drought, and of the shadow of death." It's the land that David dubbed the "valley of the shadow of death" in the twenty-third psalm.

What I've discovered so far in this strange Land is a marvelous serendipity. When I entered the Valley, things changed perceptibly. My focus was initially on my cancer. But God graciously refocused me—on my faith. Delightfully, I discovered under fire what I had always secretly hoped would be the case before the going got tough. And that is that following Jesus Christ is an adventure made more joyous, not less, by an increasingly difficult terrain. I discovered that faith in God is not merely a doughy, pietistic exercise in futility but rather the substance of things hoped for and the evidence of things not seen. I discovered that the gospel for which I had worked and sacrificed actually becomes more, not less, real. I discovered that God shows up in this place like no place else and removes the veil from my eyes, giving sight to my faith, and definitively proving that He is a very present help in time of trouble.

Alexander Solzhenitsyn famously thanked God for prison because of what God taught him there. In a similar vein and for the same reason, I thank God for the Valley. I have found that faith in this Valley draws one into a world shorn of fearful caution. While I battle the physical scourge of cancer, the life of faith teems with thrills, boldness, danger, shocks, some reversals, yes, but also triumphs and epiphanies. For the first time in my life, I find myself relating to the apostle Paul whom I behold in Scripture boldly traipsing through the known world while contemplating risky trips to what must have seemed the antipodes (Spain), shaking the dust from his sandals and worrying not about the morrow, but only the moment. I dare to imagine that's how it was for him then, so it is for me (and you) now. We are embarking on no safe journey here, but it promises not to bore.

Since I'm already here in the Valley and have been for some time, I thought I would volunteer for a new role: travel writer. I'm actually uninterested in writing for tourists and much more keen on writing for travelers. My friend Allen Arnold draws the distinction between these two admirably: "I once read a great article contrasting a tourist from a traveler. A tourist was defined as one who wanted to fly in and out, not get their hands dirty and have a largely manufactured experience. A traveler, on the other hand, came packed to stay longer and experience the environment in a more intimate way. Stay with the locals. Go off the beaten path. Come back changed rather than entertained."[2]

There's no question that I'm not writing for mere tourists in these pages. My friends, I know that you have not come to the Valley to sightsee. You have not embarked on this journey as an amusement but as a calling. You are not a tourist, but a Traveler as am I. Since I'm just a little farther along on this journey, it would be my privilege to share some tips with you in these pages that are calculated to keep you instructed and inspired.

And so I propose to send a travel report back to my old homeland where people know they're going to die someday but still insist on living like they're immortal. I affectionately refer to this homeland as Myopia because spiritually, that's what afflicted me for the fifty-three years I lived there. But now that I've arrived in the Valley, I long to share with you who come closely behind me what I have newly seen.

So Faithful Spy, that's me, your new Travel Writer, reporting from the Valley.

As an inveterate Harley-rider pastor, I value the annual Blessing of the Bikes in which my biker brothers and sisters come together to pray for God's protection, help, and blessings throughout our upcoming dangerous two-wheeled excursions. It strikes me that a similar blessing is appropriate for all of us in this even more dangerous excursion of ours through the Valley. So as we begin, please receive from me the following blessing that my friend singer/songwriter Jenny Simmons originally conferred on me (just substitute your name for "Andy") when I first entered this strange land of Cancer:

> *I pray, Andy, when you are scared, God will meet you in this foreign country. I pray, friend, that when you feel lost and homesick for the life that was, you will meet God in this foreign country. I pray, Pastor, that when you feel out of your element, when you experience culture shock, you and God will adjust in the new land, as good friends, ex-pats, in an adventure . . . for the Savior who greets us in the midst of our fear, anger, homesick, and humble new beginnings smiles, offers us a well-worn chair, and a warm but amazing Guinness and says, "Welcome home, child."*

Please know my friends that I am praying these same prayers for all of you,[3] and that I consider it a special privilege that you would allow me to walk along with you on this journey. As we go, I pray that hope will blaze in your heart, that faith will lift you, and that love will sustain you every step of the way.

Your Intrepid Travel Writer,

Pastor Andy

☼

MY FRIEND DR. LARRY PARSLEY THREW DOWN THE FOLLOWING GAUNTLET TO ME AS I BEGAN WRITING THESE MISSIVES FROM THE VALLEY:

Preachers too can learn to inspire listeners with exhibits from distant lands. We should be like the faithful spies of Numbers 13, who point to the gigantic grape clusters from the Valley of Eschol and say to the people, "There's more where that came from." Our sermons should be sprinkled with stories of faithful believers who faced down Amalekites and lived to sink their teeth into the fruit of the land. Our preaching can reassure fellow travelers that the very place, which is presently a "Valley of Weeping," can be transformed into a "place of refreshing springs" (Psalm 84:6 NLT). Or as that great travel writer John Bunyan might put it, our ultimate destination is not the "Slough of Despond, but the Celestial City."[4]

1

STORY: GOD TELLS YOURS

"THEN IT WAS YOU WHO WOUNDED ARAVIS?"
"IT WAS I."
"BUT WHAT FOR?"
"CHILD," SAID THE VOICE, VERY DEEP AND LOW SO THAT THE EARTH SHOOK, "I AM TELLING YOU YOUR STORY, NOT HERS. I TELL NO ONE ANY STORY BUT HIS OWN."[1]

My Dear Fellow Travelers,

I have described to you how I was sitting in my office minding my own business when I was interrupted by that unpleasant phone call informing me that I had been issued a personalized, gold-embossed invitation to join the cancer club.

My first reaction was "Why me?" Right when your Travel Writer was asking the "why me?" question, another Valley dweller was asking it too. In the summer of 2010 the popular author and self-professed atheist Christopher Hitchens was diagnosed with cancer. With his usual candor, he described his battle with the illness:

> *I am badly oppressed by a gnawing sense of waste. I had real plans for my next decade and felt I'd worked hard enough to earn it. Will I really not live to see my children married? To watch the World Trade*

Center rise again? . . . To the dumb question "Why me?" the cosmos barely bothers to return the reply: Why not? I sometimes wish I were suffering in a good cause, or risking my life for the good of others, instead of just being a gravely endangered patient. Allow me to inform you, though, that when you sit in a room with a set of other finalists, and kindly people bring a huge transparent bag of poison to plant into your arm [his chemotherapy treatment] and you either read or don't read a book while the venom sack gradually empties into your system . . . You feel swamped with passivity and impotence: dissolving in powerlessness like a sugar lump in water.[2]

LAMENT

Exactly, Christopher. "Why me?" Since arriving in the Valley, I've discovered that virtually everyone here has gone a round or two with that question. It's only logical that we should. It's only *biblical* that we should.

You see, God understands and encourages us to indulge our built-in need for good, old-fashioned lament. *Will I really not live to see my children married? To watch the World Trade Center rise again?* God *wants* us to acknowledge our bafflement and pain and express our distress and questions.

He *wants* us to ask with Moses, "Why have you brought this trouble on your servant?" (Numbers 11:11). God *wants* us to ask with David, "How long, Lord? Will you forget me forever? How long will you hide your face from me? How long must I wrestle with my thoughts and day after day have sorrow in my heart? How long will my enemy triumph over me?" (Psalm 13:1–2). God *wants* us to ask with Jesus, "My God, my God, why have you forsaken me?" (Matthew 27:46).

God does not fear our lament. Instead, He welcomes it. And He rues our failure to lament because that constitutes denial, which usurps the joy and ministry our heavenly Father has planned for us even in this suffering. Nearly half of the psalms (73 out of 150) have major elements of lament—God's people expressing their heartache and their prayerful pleas in the face of suffering. Why? They knew that lament prepares us to trust God's response. We cannot receive healing for unacknowledged pain or answers to unasked questions. Lament is a gift of God that is wisely utilized by His godly ones.

And so your Travel Writer lamented wholeheartedly—and continues to do so occasionally! I just wanted to know, needed to know: why? Why this? Why now? Why *me*? Was it something I did? Something I failed to do? Something *God* failed to do?

Whatever it was, the results were manifestly miserable and my heart was abjectly agitated and my prayers were brutally honest. They contained a whole lot less about what I knew—"God is great, God is good"—and a whole lot more about what I felt—"God is deaf, God is gone."

My lament was simply expressing consciously the unspoken pain in my heart. I felt this sentiment with Christopher Hitchens, "Lord, I am badly oppressed by a gnawing sense of waste!" And I spat these words to the heavens: "God, this is *me* suffering down here, hello? It appears that You have fallen down on the job and I don't like it one little bit and I wish You would get with the program and do Your duty and get me out of this jam *asap*."

Admittedly, the venting of lament was (is) a welcome relief valve. Prayerful pleas honestly expressed end in trustful hope. God designed it that way so that, having faced my predicament with eyes wide open, I can relax and, with clearer perspective, join David in this concluding prayer to his lament:

> *Look on me and answer, Lord my God. Give light to my eyes, or I will sleep in death, and my enemy will say, "I have overcome him," and my foes will rejoice when I fall. But I trust in your unfailing love; my heart rejoices in your salvation. I will sing the Lord's praise, for he has been good to me. (Psalm 13:3–6)*

As your Travel Writer, I urge you to do the same in this Valley. Let's face it. We're in a world of hurt and it's not happiness we're experiencing, but pain. God doesn't want us to pretend otherwise, but rather lament our distress honestly as a way of setting the table for experiencing His hope deeply. We will get there as we understand God's two profound answers to the "why me?" lament that all of us inevitably have: our enemy and His Story . . .

OUR REAL ENEMY

A functional knowledge of theology answers the "why me?" question at altitude for the whole human race. Why am I sick with cancer? Because cancer and all of its insidious antihuman allies of disease and disaster and death are the collateral damage of a world broken by sin at the behest of Satan, the great enemy of our souls.

An old French Huguenot pastor was once the guest preacher in a British church. His outline for a sermon on the devil that he preached was: "Who the Devil he is, What the Devil he is doing, and Where the Devil he is going!" His essential and accurate message was that what the devil is doing in this world is making war on God and on people. That reminds me that one of my nurses gave me a bumper sticker I mistakenly put on my office door to publically identify my enemy: STUPID CANCER. But I was wrong. Cancer is not my ultimate enemy—Satan is.

Cancer is just one of Satan's many tools deployed to bring death, which is the stock and trade of evil and darkness. Death is the ultimate expression of Satan's hatred toward human beings who, as creatures made in the image of God, remind him constantly of God. As the *imago dei,* we humans are "a little lower than the angels" (Psalm 8:5) now, but are destined to be revealed and exalted as God's children who will one day judge those very angels (of which Satan is but one).[3] Because in all of these ways we remind Satan so much of God, he does to us what he can't do to God, but wishes he could. If the devil can't kill God (and even he knows he can't do that), then he will settle for maiming and killing people both physically and spiritually. The devil's ultimate intention for the children of God is not good, but evil; not life, but death; not mercy, but murder.

This poses a credibility challenge to people still living in Myopia. Is the deadly opposition of the evil one difficult for you to believe? Then hear Jesus, who characterized Satan so: "He was a murderer from the beginning, not holding to the truth, for there is no truth in him" (John 8:44). Do you hear that? The primo murderer, in the history of the entire universe, is the devil. He loves to kill. There was never a time when killing wasn't pure delight to the devil. And his rap sheet shows that he has murdered *millions* of persons since the beginning of time through holocausts and abortions and disasters and yes, diseases like cancer. This puts that comical little red-suited pitchfork-packing horned putz of comic routines in a new light, doesn't it? As long as living human beings are dying in droves, Satan is one happy camper.

This is the bad old news: we human inhabitants of planet Earth have a vicious enemy who wants to murder us all both spiritually and physically in time and for eternity. But it is this dark and disturbing bad old news of Satan's murderous bloodlust that makes the good news of the gospel of Jesus Christ so beautiful.

The good news is that we have a Friend who wants to give us spiritual and physical life for time and eternity. The bad news is that Satan is a murderer.

The good news is that Jesus is the Way, the Truth, and the LIFE (John 14:6). The bad news is that the devil kills.

The good news is that Jesus saves. The bad news is that Satan wants to destroy.

The good news is that Jesus died so that you can never die. Hear His words of invitation to you and me: "I am the living bread that came down from heaven. Whoever eats this bread will live forever. This bread is my flesh, which I will give for the life of the world" (John 6:51).

Nothing is more vital in darkness than light. Nothing is more vital in death than life. And nothing makes light and life more beautiful than the occasional cancer-induced reminders that the decisive battle in spiritual warfare was fought and won by Christ at the cross and through

His resurrection. As Paul wrote, "And having disarmed the powers and authorities, he made a public spectacle of them, triumphing over them by the cross" (Colossians 2:15). In other words, Jesus has already whipped our adversary.[4]

Though we have an enemy who lands the odd withering blow, we also have a Savior who has landed Satan's death blow and nullified the evil-caused damage in time and eternity. It gives me great pleasure as your Travel Writer to remind you of these wonderful truths!

WHY ME AND NOT THEM?

Perhaps you are like me as you grapple with the "why me?" question. You are realizing that everyone suffers the collateral damage of a sin-broken world, whether through cancer or any number of other scourges wielded by the enemy of your soul. That's a theologically legitimate response that stands biblical muster. But you still have unease in your heart. The theological answer doesn't satisfy. That is when it might dawn on you as it did me that it is not the answer that is defective but the question. Perhaps we have to admit that what we're really obsessing about is not "why me?" but "why me and not *them*?"

This is an important admission for new residents of the Valley. Our adversity as cancer victims would not be so difficult nor other people's health so divisive if we felt that everybody experienced both in equal measure. But all do not and—though embarrassing to admit—the insult added to the injury of what seems to be outrageous unfairness in my life (cancer) is unusual blessing in the lives of others (health). As a result, I struggle often here in the Valley with interpreting God's treatment of me through the lens of how He treats others. I am constantly tempted to conclude that my lot in life is acceptable only if my pain is not greater nor my blessings less than those around me. And so I get on my high horse with God and demand to know, why me and not them? Maybe you have done the same thing. If so, welcome to the party!

Here's an important cause and effect relationship that I've learned

☼

TIM KELLER WRITES:

I am reminded of a line from Tolkein's *Lord of the Rings*: "The hands of the king are healing hands, and thus shall the rightful king be known." As a child blossoms under the authority of a wise and good parent, as a team flourishes under the direction of a skillful, brilliant coach, so when you come under the healing of the royal hands, under the kingship of Jesus, everything in your life will begin to heal. And when he comes back, everything sad will come untrue. His return will usher in the end of fear, suffering, and death.[5]

as your Travel Writer here in Cancerland. When I succumb to the notion that God has treated me unfairly, emotional poison flows through my veins. I become angry, bitter, and hopeless. But most devastating, my faith fails in the One whom I've effectively thrown overboard as a delinquent Deity.

To all who are secretly exercised by these unheroic yet altogether human sentiments, take heart. You're not alone! One of Christ's most prominent disciples was outspoken on the issue of comparative fairness. Simon "The Rock" Peter was an angler by trade. I think of him as the CEO of A&P Fishing Enterprises (Andrew and Peter). As an employer, Peter paid his employees' wages based on a comparison to what others of similar production levels were making. Fairness was determined by market value. That's why Peter was so interested in what Jesus told the rich young ruler in Matthew 19:21. "If you want to be perfect, go, sell your possessions and give to the poor, and you will have treasure in heaven. Then come, follow me."

When Peter heard those words, his businessman's brain engaged. If pay is determined comparatively in the physical world, why not in the spiritual? If this tightfisted young ruler had a shot at "treasure in heaven," what compensation might Peter, who had sacrificed to follow Jesus, command? Thus his question in verse 27: "We have left everything to follow you! What then will there be for us?" A rather mercenary question, wouldn't you say? Yet, do we not all raise it with God, if only subconsciously? "Lord, if I live a comparatively good Christian life, will You bless me in relation to others? And if I do more than others, will You do more for me? Can I at *least* assume that You will prevent me and my family from ever getting cancer?" Jesus' response to Peter and to us all in the Valley was the following parable from Matthew 20:1–16, which I've paraphrased:

In the Middle East, grapes were picked in September before the destructively cold and wet autumn winds came. When a certain vineyard owner saw those storms brewing, he was motivated to get his grapes in—and fast. Down to the local labor pool he went at six a.m., hired a group of workers at a denarius a day, and sent them into his fields. By nine he knew he would need more workers to finish the job, so back he went and hired more. He did the same at noon and at five p.m., giving work to men who by then had probably lost hope for employment that day.

Finally the vineyard was harvested and the workers queued up for their wages. The last group hired was paid first. They stepped up to receive pay for work begun just an hour before. These men were still fresh. Their Levis were pressed, their Doc Martens unmuddied, and their Right Guard still working! Since they'd only worked 1/12 of the day, they would have been content with a pondion, worth about 1/12 of a denarius. But to their amazement, they received the full day's pay of an entire denarius.

At first the original workers were ecstatic. As the paymaster shelled out wages, they were calculating their take: "Hey, if these one-hour guys got a denarius, surely we'll get twelve since we were here that many hours!" But their glee turned to apprehension as the next groups who had worked longer hours also received a denarius. Then came what seemed a slap in the face. When these exhausted men who had labored all day in the sweltering heat received their pay, they too were paid the same: one denarius.

An outspoken member of the first group complained bitterly about the perceived injustice. But how was it unjust? Had the employer paid the agreed-on amount? Yes. Was there a breach of contract? No. So what was wrong? Not the way the owner had treated them, but the way he had treated them in comparison with the others. He had hired them and paid what they expected. But by comparison, they had determined they deserved more than they had a right to expect.

Comparing has the same effect on us today. Especially in this Valley where the stakes are so high, we don't just want the chance to play the game, but the assurance of winning it. Jesus' timeless parable points out the foolishness of comparison, a sentiment seconded by Paul in 2 Corinthians 10:12: "We do not dare to classify or compare ourselves with some who commend themselves. When they measure themselves by themselves and compare themselves with themselves, they are not wise."

So when we come to this Valley, dwelling on the question "why me and not them?" is not a biblically recommended activity? Correct!

Why not? Let me count the ways! First, comparison destroys our gratitude to God. In Jesus' parable, poor workers who lived from hand to mouth had been given a chance to earn bread for their families. An employer had hired them for a fair wage, provided them honest work, and paid them promptly for their services. They should have been grateful. But because they measured themselves against others, they were rude, selfish, and ungrateful.

Comparison destroys our gratitude to God in the same way. A friend's business mushrooms while yours drowns in accounts receivable and you demand to know, "Why him and not me?" Childless, you leave the maternity ward where a joyful neighbor has just welcomed her third child, look up to heaven and cry, "Why her and not me?" Sure, you're glad when God does generous things for others. But oughtn't He do the same for you? Sick from chemotherapy treatments and facing an uncertain future, you crawl off the couch to attend a Bible study and pass your next-door neighbor who has not darkened the door of a church in thirty years. Why is he working on his tan while you are working to keep your supper down? Christ hasn't violated His Word when your desires aren't met, but it's tough to be grateful when the next guy's are.

But most seriously, comparing damages our relationship with God. The vineyard owner's words to the disgruntled workers have an ominous ring of finality. "Take your pay and go. I want to give the man who was hired last the same as I gave you" (Matthew 20:14). These workers' displeasure with what he had paid caused them to lose faith in him, and they probably never saw him again. He had paid them fairly, but they left in a huff because he didn't follow the rules of their comparison game. How many believers have become similarly estranged from God by interpreting His blessings to others as slights to them?

WHY NOT ME?

So if the "why me?" question is already answered and the underlying "why me and not them?" question is off-base, is there a legitimate question that we should ask upon entering the Valley that has not yet been answered and that produces gratitude and not resentment? It's perceptive of you to ask, my friend, and I'm excited to share the answer. Yes, there is a question that we Valley dwellers are wise to ask often and with enthusiasm, and that is "Why *not* me?"

This question arises from faith, not fear. It also arises from knowledge, not ignorance. "Why me?" ignorantly assumes that God was too weak to protect me from the assaults of Satan, and "Why me and not them?" ignorantly assumes that God was too distracted to treat me with equanimity. The fact is that God is neither weak nor distracted, but sovereign and good, powerful and just. King David expressed as much in his Old Testament declaration: "The Lord is gracious and righteous; our God is full of compassion. The Lord protects the unwary; when I was brought low, he saved me. Return to your rest, my soul, for the Lord has been good to you" (Psalm 116:5–7).

That means that even though we do have a virulent enemy who seeks to destroy us, we have a heavenly Father who is even more powerful who seeks to protect us. It means that even though our adversary wants to wreck our lives and render us hopeless, we have a heavenly Father who plans to make something beautiful of our lives in this Valley and give us a future for His glory. He is sovereign and therefore ultimately in control of all things, able to make even the wrath of man and the assaults of the adversary to praise Him. As the children's song so poignantly expresses it, "He holds the whole world in His hands." That is endlessly reassuring to people of faith given God's stated intent for their lives: "For I know the plans I have for you," declares the Lord, "plans to prosper you and not to harm you, plans to give you hope and a future" (Jeremiah 29:11). This has always been His blueprint for His people. As the prophet proclaimed and Jesus reiterated eight hundred years later:

> *The Spirit of the Sovereign Lord is on me, because the Lord has anointed me*
> *to proclaim good news to the poor. He has sent me to bind up the brokenhearted,*
> *to proclaim freedom for the captives and release from darkness for the prisoners, to proclaim the year of the Lord's favor and the day of vengeance of our God, to comfort all who mourn, and provide for those who grieve in Zion—*
> *to bestow on them a crown of beauty instead of ashes,*
> *the oil of joy instead of mourning,*
> *and a garment of praise instead of a spirit of despair. They will be called oaks of righteousness, a planting of the Lord*
> *for the display of his splendor.* (Isaiah 61:1–3)

The unique hope that we followers of Christ have upon entering Cancerland is that God is not only able to make this a beautiful journey for us, but that He plans to make it so. All we have to do is to stop fearing and start trusting, stop comparing and start anticipating. Because we know that our sovereign heavenly Father and not Satan calls the shots for His children, we can predict that something beautiful is going to come of this journey because of the One who makes "all things work together for good to them that love God, to them who are the called according to his purpose" (Romans 8:28 KJV).

In this vein, Jesus' parable suggests that there is a superior alternative to seeing what others are getting (or not getting, e.g., cancer) and demanding the same for ourselves. That is to trust our God to do the right thing, the best thing, and the good thing in our lives, not in

☼

AS THE GREAT CHURCH FATHER
ST. AUGUSTINE OBSERVED:

Great is the work of God,
exquisite in all he wills! so
that, in a manner wondrous
and ineffable, that is not done
without his will which is done
contrary to it, because it could
not be done if he did not permit;
nor does he permit it unwillingly,
but willingly; nor would he who
is good permit evil to be done,
were he not omnipotent to bring
good out of evil.[6]

spite of our cancer, but *through* it. Did you notice that the later groups of workers in Jesus' parable had no agreement for pay? They labored on the basis of trust in the owner's simple promise in verse 4: "He told them to go to work in his vineyard and he would pay them "whatever is right." These workers didn't stipulate demands for wage rates, or unionize, or negotiate a contract. They simply placed themselves in the master's hands, believing he would do right by them. God calls us to trust Him here in the Valley in the same way.

Such trust may be tough, but it makes sense to people in the Valley. First, because the vineyard owner, who represents God in Jesus' parable, would go back time and again to hire workers, even at the eleventh hour. Why hire guys to work only one hour? Could he really hope to gain that much from their limited labor? No. He hired those men because he cared for them. He hired them, not because he needed them, but because they needed him. That's why he gave them big pay for little work.

In the same way, God cares for you. The comparison game will make you wonder if God cares for you when your life doesn't go well. You question His love if others seem more blessed than you. But you don't know what God may be doing in the lives of others through His generosity, and you don't know what He may be doing in your life through testing. The Lord is about the business of grafting godliness into the character of His people. It's a vast oversimplification of His ways to expect that He must treat everyone equally.

In Jesus' parable those who demanded a particular wage got exactly what they requested and not a mite more. But those who trusted the master got far more than they could have imagined. That is what Jesus meant when He said, "So the last will be first, and the first will be last." Those who aggressively demand from God will someday be surprised to find themselves behind those who simply trusted Him. An old saying goes that God gives His best to those who leave the choice with Him. When that happens, we can fully appreciate the marvelous mosaic His grace is creating in our lives. We will stop existing to keep up with the Joneses and start living out the unique story of salvation God is spinning in our own experience, even our experience in this Valley of the Shadow of Death.

Do you have faith in the story God has for you? When you come to this Valley, you will want to have faith in this story! Do you believe that Christ is with you now and always, guiding your steps in the Valley and straightening your way through the Shadow? He is. He is the Master of the vineyard who responds to trust, not demand. He is the Author of our salvation who delights in weaving an utterly unique and beautiful story in each believer's life.

But to comprehend His work, we must be willing to reject all comparisons. Evidently, this was a difficult challenge for Peter. It was his self-absorbed "what's in it for me" question that elicited Jesus' parable, but unfortunately Peter didn't grasp Jesus' full meaning in it. Not long after, he was still comparing his life with others in deciding if God was fair. We see this in his last conversation with Christ who said to him:

> *"Very truly, I tell you, when you were younger you dressed yourself and went where you wanted; but when you are old you will stretch out your hands, and someone else will dress you and lead you where you do not want to go." Jesus said this to indicate the kind of death by which Peter would glorify God. Then he said to him, "Follow me!" Peter turned and saw that the disciple whom Jesus loved was following them. (This was the one who had leaned back against Jesus at the supper and had said, "Lord, who is going to betray you?") When Peter saw him, he asked, "Lord, what about him?" Jesus answered, "If I want him to remain alive until I return, what is that to you? You must follow me." (John 21:18–22)*

I can understand Peter's curiosity. He's just been told how he will die. Can we blame him for wondering if his friends faced a similar fate? But when he asked about John, Jesus' reply is blunt: "None of your business, Peter! I tell no one any story but his own." This time, Peter understood. The Lord doesn't issue cookie-cutter callings. When Peter got his eyes off others and accepted God's unique work in his own life, the greatest chapters of his story unfolded.

God is writing a bestseller, and you are His coauthor. Your history is the plotline, your experiences the setting, your faith responses the dramatic tension. Insisting that He craft your story to mirror that of others is a demand for monotony.

So many heroes of the faith—Joseph, Daniel, Ruth, Esther . . . the hall of famers in Hebrews 11—allowed the Divine Writer to finish His story in their lives even if, for some of them, it meant not receiving earthly deliverance. Each received God's best because they left the choice with Him. Each trusted until every sentence was crafted, every paragraph polished, every chapter completed ". . . that they might obtain a better resurrection." Won't you do the same? The result will be yet another masterpiece. It's always too soon to quit if God is in the picture. As Paul reminds us in 1 Corinthians 2:9 NLT, "However, as it is written: 'No eye has seen, no ear has heard, no mind has imagined what God has prepared for those who love him.'" I have become fond of quoting that promise to myself every time I sit down in the chemo lab. My endurance is bolstered by knowing that each drip from that poisonous IV is just a new sentence in a pretty darn good tale that my heavenly Father is spinning about my life.

God is the Maker, the Master of new things, the Singer of new songs. Don't insult His creativity by asking Him to plagiarize old stories. In your experience in this Valley, God is creating something special. Trust Him to do a good job. So when He introduces a dramatic element into your story that includes cancer, just ask enthusiastically the rhetorical question, "Why *not* me?" No matter how bleak your prospects, no matter how blessed your peers, be assured that if Christ is your King, every heartache is but a new chapter in your story. Never forget: in a masterpiece, every chapter is not only elegant, but essential. Let the Almighty Author finish!

Jesus tells no one anyone's story but their own. Those latecomer workers in the vineyard listened. Peter and all those biblical heroes listened. I'm listening. And I pray you will listen, too. And the proof for all of us that we are indeed listening as Jesus tells us each our own story will be our often asking of a similar-sounding but actually quite different new question . . .

Your "Why NOT Me?"
Travel Writer,

Pastor Andy

2

IMMANUEL: GOD IS WITH YOU

THE CHRISTIAN FAITH ENABLES US TO FACE LIFE OR MEET DEATH, NOT BECAUSE WE CAN SEE, BUT WITH THE CERTAINTY THAT WE ARE SEEN; NOT THAT WE KNOW ALL THE ANSWERS, BUT THAT WE ARE KNOWN.[1]

My Dear Traveling Friends,

It's a wonderful thing to feel flush with faith in God. To observe the evidences of His reality, to marvel at the wisdom of His Word, and best of all, to see His hand working good things in our lives is pure joy. From the Valley today I have good news and bad news. The bad news is—it's not always like that over here. The good news is—it's not supposed to be. Joy in our Christian walk is a major part of God's plan, but know this: the desert is also an integral part of His design for our time in the Valley.

The desert is a metaphor for those spiritually thirsty seasons in our lives when we're discouraged or struggling, when things are going downhill, when we're hurt or sick or we've failed God or, even worse, when we think He's failed us. We pray, but it seems our requests bounce off the ceiling. We study God's Word, but it seems dry and irrelevant.

We still believe in God, but we wonder if He still believes in us. We still love God, but we're troubled because we can't understand Him.

Once we would spring out of bed with a "Good morning, God!" But now in the desert sometimes we barely manage to pry open our eyelids and sit up dejectedly: "Good God, it's morning." Especially on chemo weeks, that's definitely my own standard modus operandi.

Along with chemotherapy, one of my regular portals to the desert experience in this Valley is the dreaded clipboard.

THE CLIPBOARD KING

Valley dwellers know that each time they go to a new doctor (and often when they return to see their regular doctor), they get a clipboard of forms to fill out before they're even allowed to dream of entering the actual examination room. They have been long disabused of the reasonable assumption that having thoroughly filled out one medical clipboard, doctors would share the information and relieve you of filling out the same information over and over again in different offices. No, that would be entirely too easy. A new clipboard must always be completed, world without end, AMEN. Valley dwellers know they must also do this same clipboard dance before they check into a hospital or have any sort of scan or medical procedure. It's just the way every waiting room rolls, which is why I question it being called a waiting room at all. It's more like a project room. You're not waiting, you're clipboarding!

Well, I confess it's getting to me. When I lived in Myopia, I did the clipboard thing every once in a while with long separations in between. But my acceptance into the Cancer Club has necessitated the filling out of no less than thirteen clipboards' worth of forms in the last month alone. This is a dizzying assault of bureaucratic bullies, of administrative assassins, of finger-cramping, mind-numbing silliness. Perhaps you can relate.

I've got a new oncologist, a urologist, a colonoscopy doc, and two new surgeons—all with clipboards. I've had a CT scan, a PET scan, and a mediport surgically installed—all requiring clipboards. Add to that one a new heart doctor (another clipboard) who put me through no less than three scanning procedures to check for blocked arteries (three new clipboards), and another heart scan from yet another doc (two new clipboards), and in the last two years it all adds up to many clipboards' worth of repetitious, monotonous, mundane, unpleasant information. Did I say thirteen before? I was wrong. It is worse than I thought. If you feel like pushing me over the emotional edge just to see what a raving, maniacal pastor on chemo looks like, just smile and hand me a clipboard. I'm not responsible for what might happen next.

I know what you're thinking. "Chill Andy, it's just a little bit of information they want. What's the big deal? Write it down and move on." Don't be so reasonable. Someday you might find yourself buried under a clipboard avalanche, and we'll see how chipper you are to inscribe yet one more unmerciful form.

It's not that what the clipboards demand to know is unreasonable. It's that you are required to recite the same information over and over again without respite. Name. Address. Phone. Emergency contact. Their phone. Primary physician. Phone. Address (who knows their doctor's address, for Pete's sake?!). Insurance company. Phone. Group number. Address (like I know that!). Supplemental insurance company. Phone. Group number. Address. Next of kin. Age. Phone. Children. Their Ages. Their phone numbers. Your net worth. Your bank account number in case your insurance doesn't pay up. The bank's phone. Address (naturally).

That's just the first page.

The next several pages of the clipboard have to do with your entire medical life history. Whole lists of maladies to check if you have them, spaces to write in all the medicines you are taking, ever took, or might take, blanks to record every surgery or medical procedure you've ever had and the date you had it on and the doctor who performed it (phone number please!) and the hospital where it happened and the phone number and address of said hospital and what color were the nurses' scrubs in the operating room on that day? (Okay, I made up that last one, but only that one!)

Now that you've painfully rehearsed every low medical moment of your life, it's time to sign those mandatory release forms. These spell out in morbid detail everything that could go wrong with your upcoming treatment. You are invited to sign the form inviting the medical community to inflict any of these unappealing outcomes upon you with your full legal consent.

Your humble Travel Writer has not yet told you the most infuriating thing about the clipboard, though. On every page, you must write your name at the top. Not just initials, but the whole thing on every page. One day I was doing a fourteen-page-long clipboard form when I rebelliously pulled a *Braveheart,* bellowed, "Freedom!" (albeit silently), and turned it all in to Nurse Ratched without affixing my name to every single page. She clearly regarded me as one attempting to fly over the cuckoo's nest because she fixed a steely eye on me as if to say, "Nice try, doofus, but you're not getting this past me." She then did actually say, "Sir, please write your name at the top of each page." As smoothly and evenly as I could I intoned, "But my full name and attendant information is clearly inscribed on the very first page. Mightn't that be enough?" With a derogatory roll of the eyes she sighed, "No, just please go back and write your name thirteen more times." I caved and did it. I am so not Braveheart. Mel Gibson aka William Wallace would have mooned that receptionist, hewed that clipboard asunder with his sword, and stormed out to slay some recalcitrant Englishmen. Me? I just meekly wrote and rewrote my name like a pitiful sophomore in detention hall.

WHERE IS YOUR GOD?

See why this is getting to me?

I think it has something to do with the essential message that these endless clipboards seem to be sending: "You are unknown, and therefore on your own." To be in community is to be known. To be alone is to be unknown. Thus the clipboards are saying that, because apparently everything about me is perennially unknown (and must be recommunicated endless times), I am essentially alone.

Welcome to the desert! Here you're not just thirsty. You're lonely too. You are not just in the Valley; you're in the Valley by yourself. Nobody remembers who you are or why you are here. Even God seems distant. What did you say your name was again? Please write it again on every page. Is anybody home here? God, have you exited this Valley too?

What is it that makes us long to be known? The theme song to *Cheers* affirms that universal desire: "You want to be where everybody knows your name."[2]

Sure you do. Sure we all do! That was actually C. S. Lewis's philosophy of books. "We read to know we are not alone." The inimitable Mr. Lewis is right. We want to know people's troubles are all the same, as the iconic *Cheers* theme points out. But the song reveals that there's more: We don't want to be unknown because we don't want to feel alone.

That's why "Tabitha" graffitied her name on a high wall in Blarney Castle over the date 1754. That's why the Count of Monte Cristo scratched his name into his cell wall at Chateau D'If. That's why a GI in WW2, after having peered over a wall to see if the Germans were coming, scrawled on it the famous words "Kilroy was here." That's why I carved my name on my wooden desktop in Mrs. Tully's second grade classroom (back when carrying a pocketknife to school wouldn't get you in trouble).

"Kilroy was here" wasn't a silly attempt to intimidate the enemy. Kilroy wrote that because he wanted someone to know that a real person with real troubles and a real life had been in that spot. Just writing it comforted Kilroy just as it did Tabitha and Edmond Dantès and seven-year-old Andy. In the writing of their names they were identifying themselves, and there is just something in the human spirit that deeply

☼

Ever try to watch a seed grow? You can't. It's hidden in the soil until the seedling breaks the surface and appears. Then you realize that even though you couldn't see it, something grand has been happening in that hidden place. In the desert part of this Valley, we need to trust that the same God who *has* helped us, *will* help us. The same God we have known, we will know. The same God we have loved, we will love even more. We simply need to take God at His word when he says, "I am making a way in the wilderness and streams in the wasteland" (Isaiah 43:19).

desires simply to be known so as not to feel all alone. "God, even as I'm writing my name at the top of every page of every clipboard, I'm just letting you know I'm walking through this desert in this Valley." ANDY WAS HERE.

But I also desperately want to know . . . are You? I would especially like to know that right about now. Are You present in this Valley with me? I daresay everybody here is keen to know the answer to that question.

In Psalm 42:1–2, David puts words to the loneliness that many travelers feel here in this desert valley. "As the deer pants for streams of water, so my soul pants for you, my God. My soul thirsts for God, for the living God." That's deep, soul-felt thirst. David is in the desert, longing to sense the closeness and encouragement of God. Thus the panting—ongoing thirst for the assurance of a God who seems absent. As Verla Gillmor put it: "Not too long ago, it seemed as though God had packed up, moved far away, and left me no forwarding address. I was unable to sense his promptings and overall presence as I searched for him during trying times. I felt abandoned, confused, and terribly alone."[3]

If you've been a Christian for any length of time, I know you've felt that. If you're now in the cancer club, I'm certain you have felt that, right along with me. Let's face it. In this desert valley of mortal danger, it's hard not to feel trampled, brokenhearted, and worst of all, alone. Each one of those fourteen clipboards has shouted that same response to my heart so much so that I can easily echo King David's words: "My tears have been my food day and night, while people say to me all day long, 'Where is your God?'" (Psalm 42:3).

Where is He, indeed. Historically, God's people have often been taunted with these very words. From Jesus on the cross to Paul in a Philippian jail to Christians in Nero's Coliseum, people of faith have always been derided with these words when times were tough. "Where is your God?" The worst part is that such jabs cause doubt in our own hearts and prod us to ask, "Where *is* my God?" If you've recently asked that question upon entering the Valley, you're in good company.

King David, man after God's own heart, asked it. Righteous Job asked it. Fleeing Jonah asked it. Jeremiah, the Weeping Prophet, asked it. Pursued by the wicked Jezebel, Elijah asked it. John the Baptizer, the greatest among men according to Jesus, asked it from Herod's dungeon. Jesus Himself asked it from the cross: "My God, why have You forsaken Me?"

Here is what we must conclude from these biblical examples: all of God's children are sometimes schooled in the desert of God's seeming absence. As we've seen, even the Lord Jesus Christ wasn't spared the desert experience. So don't panic if you find yourself in the desert. It's just part of the Valley. Everyone goes there sometimes.

REMEMBRANCE

The operative question then is what do we do when we are up to our eyeballs in clipboards and desert Valley loneliness? We do what David did. He remembered.

> *These things I remember as I pour out my soul: how I used to go to the house of God under the protection of the Mighty One with shouts of joy and praise among the festive throng. Why, my soul, are you downcast? Why so disturbed within me? Put your hope in God, for I will yet praise him, my Savior and my God. My soul is downcast within me; therefore I will remember you . . . (Psalm 42:4–6)*

I remember, David says, the joy and thanksgiving I felt toward God in happier times. The Hebrew here literally says, "I *will* remember," a strong expression of determination to remember the joy that God's presence granted him in the past.

The Israelites were notoriously inept at remembrance. No matter how many miracles God did for them, it was never enough. They complained about the Egyptians, so God parted the Red Sea and granted them a miracle of escape. But they soon forgot and complained again. This time, they were thirsty in the desert, so God caused water to spring from a rock and miraculously refresh the people. But they soon forgot and complained again. They were hungry and the manna God fed them wasn't enough. So miraculously God brought them quail and they enjoyed a Texas-sized barbeque. But they soon forgot when they saw the fortified cities in Canaan they would have to assault. God said He would give them victory, but they didn't trust Him and turned away only to wander for forty years in the desert. They forgot the parting of the sea, they forgot the water from the rock, they forgot the manna in the wilderness, and they forgot the quail. No wonder David is determined to remember!

So must we be! What do you need to remember about God's goodness to you in the past before you ever even saw one of those infernal clipboards? Did He never give you hope when everything around you shouted despair? Has He never seen you through a difficult passage or sprung you from a tight spot? Some people have a bad habit of remembering only the illnesses, accidents, and layoffs while forgetting the restorative healing, miraculous provision, remarkable "coincidences," eternal blessings. When we do this, are we not acting just like the forgetful Israelites? Blocking out God's goodness not only dishonors Him, it weakens us. But remembering His goodness sharpens our sense of His presence.

HE'S IN THE DESERT

As your Travel Writer, I know that though God's past faithfulness is nice, now is now and it sure would be nice to actually hear from Him! God's sometimes silence in this Valley is painful. But by faith, please affirm that silence doesn't mean stagnation. Just because you can't see or hear Him right now does not mean God has checked out or given up on you. It most certainly does not mean He is not with you.

Even in his desert, David believed that, so he was able to say, "I will yet praise Him." But when, David? you might ask. How long will God's silence last? It takes as long as it takes—and it will seem dark and lonely the whole time. But if you pay close attention, you will find that the desert is a great

☼

AS CO-VALLEY DWELLER AND HARVARD LAW PROFESSOR WILLIAM J. STUNTZ WRITES:

"Our God remembers even his most forgettable children. But that memory is not the dry, lifeless thing we feel when one or another old friend comes to mind . . . In the Bible, remembrance usually combines two meanings: first, holding the one who is remembered close in the heart, and second, acting on the memory. When God repeatedly tells the people of Israel to remember that he brought them out of Egypt, he is saying much more than 'get your history right.' A better paraphrase would go like this: 'Remember that I have loved you passionately. Remember that I have acted on that love. Hold tight to that memory, and act on it too.'"[4]

place to listen for God's voice in ways you've never heard it before. Like David in Psalm 42:7–8: "Deep calls to deep in the roar of your waterfalls; all your waves and breakers have swept over me. By day the Lord directs his love, at night his song is with me—a prayer to the God of my life."

Near Mount Hermon at the head of the Jordan River, David could hear the waterfalls and thundering cataracts of that mountainous region. In their power and might, they seemed to be calling to one another, "deep unto deep." But they also called to David. In the quiet and solitude of that place, David meditated on the greatness and power of God and was refreshed. Panting in the heat and thirst of the desert, David welcomed God's waves as they swept over him.

Even in the silence, God's handiwork in creation shouts to our listening ears. The moon calls to the deeps in the sea, raising the tides twice a day. The sun and the rain call to the deeps in a seed, causing it to stir with life and spring up and grow. Vast distances call to the deeps in wild birds, enticing them to wing their way across trackless wastes to lay their eggs. Voices call to certain fish, sending them across the seas to spawn.

Just because we land in the desert doesn't mean that the miracles of life cease. It's just that they become more challenging for us to detect. But listen carefully, and you'll hear and see them everywhere. King David did, and so he concluded something about the Lord:

> *Where can I go from your Spirit? Where can I flee from your presence? . . . If I settle on the far side of the sea, even there your hand will guide me, your right hand will hold me fast. If I say, "Surely the darkness will hide me and the light become night around me," even the darkness will not be dark to you. (Psalm 139: 7, 9–12)*

So my friends please consider this: Silence is not absence. God may appear to be silent in your desert, but He is relentlessly faithful whether you realize it or not.

I have read that certain Native Americans had a unique way of training young braves who had mastered their hunting and fishing skills.

☼

We cannot think Him distant who sustains us each instant. Remembering God reminds us that He remembers us. So while you are here in the Valley, don't forget to remember! Present hardships notwithstanding, because God has been faithful in your past, you can trust Him for your future.

On the night of a boy's thirteenth birthday, he faced one final test. He had to spend the entire night alone in a dense forest. Until then, he had never been away from the security of his family and tribe. But on this night, he was blindfolded, led miles away, and left at night in thick woods. Imagine the terror even a twig snapping must have evoked. But when dawn broke the boy would see a man standing in the shadows just feet away, armed with bow and arrow. It was his father, who had been standing guard all through that long and frightful night.

Whether you realize it or not, God is doing the same thing for you in the Valley because that is just what He has always done for His people in the desert. Moses reminded the Israelites of this when they were disposed to forget it. "The Lord your God has . . . watched over your journey through this vast wilderness. These forty years the Lord your God has been with you, and you have not lacked anything" (Deuteronomy 2:7).

Consider Jesus' disciples alone in a boat at night at His behest. Caught there in the Valley of a howling storm, they were terrified for their very lives. Surely someone lamented, "Why did Jesus send us out here to perish by ourselves?" But if that is what they thought, they were wrong. They were never alone. Jesus had not forsaken them, and His faithfulness to them had not diminished one whit in the storm: "He saw the disciples straining at the oars, because the wind was against them. Shortly before dawn he went out to them, walking on the lake" (Mark 6:48).

Here in the Valley, Christ's disciples continue to experience God's presence with us in the midst of the storm. Randy Alcorn recalls when a friend, writer Ethel Herr, had a double mastectomy. Two months later doctors discovered that the cancer had spread. One of Herr's friends, shocked and fumbling for words, asked her, "and how do you feel about God now?" Reflecting on the moment the question was posed to her, Herr says:

> *As I sought to explain what has happened in my spirit, it all became clearer to me. God has been preparing me for this moment. He has undergirded me in ways I've never known before. He has made himself increasingly real and precious to me. He has given to me joy such as*

☼

WILLIAM STUNTZ SAYS,

"Philosophers and scientists and law professors (my line of work) are not in the best position to understand the Christian story. Musicians and painters and writers of fiction are much better situated—because the Christian story is a story, not a theory or an argument, and definitely not a moral or legal code. Our faith is, to use C. S. Lewis's apt words, the myth that became fact. Our faith is a painting so captivating that you cannot take your eyes off it. Our faith is a love song so achingly beautiful that you weep each time you hear it. At the center of that true myth, that painting, that song, stands a God who does vastly more than remember his image in us. He pursues us as lovers pursue one another. It sounds too good to be true, and yet it is true. So I have found, in the midst of pain and heartache and cancer."[5]

I've never known before—and I've no need to work at it, it just comes, even amidst the tears. He has taught me that no matter how good my genes are or how well I take care of my diet and myself, he will lead me on whatever journey he chooses and will never leave me for a moment of that journey. And he planned it all in such a way that step by step, he prepared me for the moment when the doctor dropped the last shoe . . . God is good, no matter what the diagnosis or the prognosis, or the fearfulness of the uncertainty of having neither. The key to knowing God is good is simply knowing him.[6]

I know that here in the Valley you will be tempted to think Jesus has left you, and I want to assure you that He has not. In fact, He cannot, for He has promised: "Never will I leave you; never will I forsake you" (Hebrews 13:5b). Herein is the faithfulness of Jesus Christ: not that He spares us storms in life, but that He sees us every moment we are in those storms and He comes to us in powerful and wonderful ways in the middle of those storms. He does not keep us from storms, but walks with us through them: "When you pass through the waters, I will be with you; and when you pass through the rivers, they will not sweep over you. When you walk through the fire, you will not be burned; the flames will not set you ablaze" (Isaiah 43:2). Wizened veterans of the Valley know this is true and gently cajole the rest of us therefore to relax in the presence of God.

PRAISE IN THE DESERT

So God, are You here . . . in this Valley? Oh yes, He's here, leading every step of the way. I am known and therefore never alone. So I'm thinking that maybe at a metaphysical level I'm making too much out of those accursed clipboards. (But maybe not!) All I know is that they have produced in me a wonder and delight at something about God that I've never before truly appreciated as I should. Though in this Valley I may be just a number or statistic or demographic, to God I am intimately,

☼

Be at peace. Do not look forward in fear to the changes of life; rather look to them with full hope as they arise. God, whose very own you are, will deliver you from out of them. He has kept you hitherto, and He will lead you safely through all things; and when you cannot stand it, God will bury you in His arms. Do not fear what may happen tomorrow; the same everlasting Father who cares for you today will take care of you then and every day. He will either shield you from suffering or will give you unfailing strength to bear it. Be at peace and put aside all anxious thoughts and imaginations.[7]

thoroughly, and compassionately known as a real person. And that means I'm never alone. Never. And neither are you no matter how bad it gets. The irony is, it took clipboard despair to teach me that. I had to feel alone in the Valley before I could gain confidence that God never left me alone there.

That God has searched me and sees me and perceives my thoughts from afar when people and government and banks and even next-door neighbors aren't really aware of my existence is just too wonderful. That God is with me and around me and understands my heart and my hurts and my ways and my words when it seems the world doesn't give a flying rip about any of that is just too lofty for me to attain.

So I don't have to carve my name in a desktop or scratch it on a wall or carve it into a stone to be known. I am known by the One who, in His knowing of me, brings peace and comfort and hope here in the Valley. He knows my name and He's glad I came. You too! So we can see our troubles are all the same and that's no big deal because God is here in this Valley, His hand guiding us, His right hand holding us fast.

And the best part? Heaven has no clipboards.

Your "Clipboard King"
Travel Writer,

Pastor Andy

3

BELIEVE: PRAY ACCORDINGLY

☼

DEVOTE YOURSELVES TO PRAYER, BEING WATCHFUL AND THANKFUL. —COLOSSIANS 4:2

MORE THINGS ARE WROUGHT BY PRAYER THAN THIS WORLD DREAMS OF. WHEREFORE, LET THY VOICE RISE LIKE A FOUNTAIN FOR ME NIGHT AND DAY. FOR WHAT ARE MEN BETTER THAN SHEEP OR GOATS THAT NOURISH A BLIND LIFE WITHIN THE BRAIN, IF, KNOWING GOD, THEY LIFT NOT HANDS OF PRAYER, BOTH FOR THEMSELVES AND THOSE WHO CALL THEM FRIEND? FOR SO THE WHOLE ROUND EARTH IS EVERY WAY BOUND BY GOLD CHAINS ABOUT THE FEET OF GOD.
—ALFRED, LORD TENNYSON

Dear Fellow Travelers,

A really good thing to do here in the Valley is pray. A much appreciated and popular thing here in the Valley is to get prayed for (sorry for the hanging preposition, but it just needs to hang right there . . .).

I learned this unforgettably when the IBC (Irving Bible Church) staff gets me this pager and puts the number out on the website and to our missionaries around the world and in weekend services for people to call when they pray for me. It vibrates violently each time someone dials in. It does not tell me who is calling or what they prayed, only that they just finished praying for me. I got home from a short vacation last Friday and found it waiting for me, sitting impatiently on the hope chest in our living room, buzzing like a banshee. It buzzed through supper, the evening news, a rerun of *Harry Potter*, the *Tonight Show*, and on into the night. At 2:30 a.m., it was still buzzing on the desk in my study next door and keeping me awake. How insensitive of people to be praying for me at such an ungodly hour!

Of course, I jest (on that last point only—the rest, amazingly, is true). I have had that pager on my person now for several months. Around the clock, it never stops buzzing. I have found that I can get a passably good massage by holding it at various angles to my neck and shoulders. Sometimes multiple people call simultaneously, producing extralong buzzes. I like that. It is better than the spa. Who needs a masseuse when instead you can have God's people interceding for you?

My doctors wondered why I am doing so well after major surgery. The reason is simple. Prayer works. As Charles Spurgeon said, "Prayer is able to prevail with heaven and bend omnipotence to its desire." So it is. And so an idea came to me. The next time I spoke at IBC, I thanked everyone for their prayers and for the encouragement of paging me every time they prayed. Then I asked a special favor. "Going forward, when you pray for me and buzz the pager, will you also pray for everyone who is with me right then?" Hundreds of faces clouded in puzzlement nodded yes and I thanked them profusely.

The very next day I was back in the waiting room at the chemo lab, chatting with a newly tattooed acquaintance who looked like a recently minted member of the Hell's Angels. For the first time, I had set the pager out on the end table and it buzzed incessantly, annoying my new friend as he tried to carry on a conversation. "Dude," he asked, "you gonna answer that thing?" "No," I said. "I do not answer it. I just get encouraged by hearing it buzz."

The quizzical look on his face demanded further explanation. "When my friends pray, they buzz that pager to let me know they said a prayer for me."

"That's cool," he said.

"Well, there's more," I said. "I have asked my friends to not just pray for me when they buzz this pager, but also for everyone who is with me."

Just then, the pager went off and without missing a beat I said, "Yes indeed, you just got prayed for." After I spoke, I noticed it had become quiet in the waiting room and I looked up to see twenty-five other sets of eyes fastened hopefully on me. "Yep, you too!" I told them. "You *all* just got prayed for!" You could detect a palpable sense of relief in that entire room when I made that declaration. Everybody in the Valley covets prayer, but not everybody receives it. That is why they are especially grateful when they do. I know I am.

For eighteen months that pager went off twenty-four/seven. And I took it with me to every doctor's office and hospital and chemo lab I frequented so that now I doubt there is a physician or nurse in northeast Texas who does not know and appreciate the story of that numinous pager. Everybody loves to know they've been prayed for, even if they are not sick, even if they are doctors and nurses. Like I said, prayer is a very popular thing here in the Valley. Even for recently minted members of the Hell's Angels.

For obvious reasons, people here in the Valley need to pray and be prayed for like never before. Jesus is the Great Physician, and we are very sick, and so we pray for healing. We pray to get through the surgeries and chemo. We pray for strength. We pray for God's help. We pray for life. We've always needed to pray and be prayed for even before we entered the Valley. It is just that now we see it more clearly than those still in the land of Myopia. Our need births our prayers. And so I wrote these words to my friends:

Here is why I am counting on your prayers. I've got a pretty bad cancer and the next two to three months are crucial in determining how much longer I'm going to have to deal with traffic jams, high income taxes, and smarmy politicians on this planet. Oncologists rank the seriousness of the disease in stages, one being least serious and four being barely hanging on. Various scans and pathology reports coming out of the last surgery indicate that I now occupy that fourth barely hanging-on stage. Those evil little devils (can I call cancer cells devils? I just did. Actually, I originally used a stronger word, which Alice made me take out) have spread to a lymph node near my aorta and right next to my spine where they are sassing the doctors and sticking their insolent little tongues out at us every time we snap their picture.

Here's how we are going to attack. I start six months of chemotherapy next Wednesday, August 26. Two or three months in, we'll take another picture to see if the cancer in that lymph node is dead. If not, another major surgery—we yank the sucker out of there and then continue chemo. If so—and this is the option we all pray for, okay?—we just finish the chemo, test to see that all the other cancer is dead, and I live on to teach my grandchildren how to hit high fades and low hooks off the fairway. So just to reiterate: we are praying that the High Lord God of the Universe might deign to use the tool of chemo to zap those cancer demons right out of this pastor's whole body over the next six months starting next Wednesday. Got it? Good (and thanks!).

I guess while I'm at it, I may as well ask you also to pray me through the chemo. As so many of you out there who have endured this drudgery can surely attest, it actually has the makings of a very interesting time for relationships in my life. The top three side effects they've warned me about are extreme fatigue, nausea, and diarrhea. I am hoping to be able to work at IBC somewhat normally through these months, but I hope you'll understand if, during that time when I'm in conversation with you, I suddenly fall asleep, blow groceries, or dash off to the men's room. It is nothing personal. Really. Another weird side effect is neuropathy (numbness or pain in mouth, throat, fingers) if I drink or handle anything cold while on chemo. So I can only drink warm Guinness and have no ice in my tea and I have to wear gloves if I take anything out of the fridge. I am not making this up! But hey, they tell me I can keep my hair, so all is not lost (literally)!

Just because prayer is important to us Valley dwellers does not necessarily mean we know how to do it. That is a problem because, for many of us, entering the Valley was the very first time we ever asked any serious questions about prayer. If we ever needed to know how and what and when to pray effectively, now is that time. It is our very lives we are interceding for here, and messing up in our prayers is simply not an option.

So are there prayer instruction manuals I can buy? Is there a tried-and-true technique for praying I can master? You can watch workouts—remember *Buns of Steel?* How about something on praying called *Knees of Tungsten?* We need some help, because sometimes prayer can be a bit of a puzzle, especially for those of us in the Valley.

THE "WHAT" OF PRAYER

We wonder, are we supposed to pray for healing with bold confidence that God has promised to make us well if only we have enough faith? Or do we pray more tentatively that God's will simply be done, whatever that is? What do we ask for, what ought we to ask for, and how do we ask for what we ask? And what ought our expectations be of what God does with our prayers? Is He obligated to do what we say, or are we just lobbing faintly hopeful wishes toward heaven?

The good news is that Jesus' own disciples had many of these same questions about prayer. In Luke 11, they observed Jesus practicing prayer with even greater mastery and power than Rory McElroy hitting a golf ball. It made them want to pray powerfully as well: "One day when Jesus was praying in a certain place . . . one of his disciples said to him, 'Lord, teach us to pray, just as John taught his disciples'" (Luke 11:1).

In verses 2–4, Jesus obliged them by teaching them the "what" of prayer: "Father, hallowed be your name, your kingdom come. Give us each day our daily bread. Forgive us our sins, for we forgive everyone who sins against us. And lead us not into temptation." These thematic statements represent the "what" of prayer—simple to understand categories of honoring and submitting to God and His kingdom and also making intercession for our needs.

But as we've noted, the real problem is not understanding the "what," but the "how" of prayer. So I'm glad that Jesus immediately taught His disciples (and us!) *how* to pray *what* they prayed by unveiling the following three principles for powerful prayer. As your faithful Travel Writer, I want you to have them because I have found that they come in especially handy here in the Valley.

THE "HOW" OF PRAYER

1. Pray Persistently

> *Then Jesus said to them, "Suppose you have a friend, and you go to him at midnight and say, 'Friend, lend me three loaves of bread; a friend of mine on a journey has come to me, and I have no food to offer him.' And suppose the one inside answers, 'Don't bother me. The door is already locked, and my children and I are in bed. I can't get up and give you anything.' I tell you, even though he will not get up and give you the bread because of friendship, yet because of your shameless audacity he will surely get up and give you as much as you need. (Luke 11:5–8)*

A typical one-room Palestinian house of Jesus' day was divided into two parts: the loft and the main floor. At night, families would bring livestock inside, turning the main floor into a stable. The family ate and slept in the loft. So this guy is upstairs in the loft with his sleeping wife and kids, the animals are in the living room, the late night guy just signed off, and all is quiet on the western front. Just then, his friend comes by and calls out he wants to borrow some chips and dip to entertain over at his place. If I were this guy, I would not exactly welcome a visit at that hour, friend or no friend, would you? You have to get up, crawl over your sleeping family, find the ladder, negotiate it in the dark, and then pick your way barefoot across a minefield (by virtue of the livestock) in your living room. No wonder he said, "Get lost!"

But the friend did not get lost. Instead, he raised the decibel level in imploring, "How 'bout those chips 'n' dip?" The homeowner, who by now was wishing he had opted for the gated community, hissed, "Get lost, I said!" At that, the persistent neighbor went to the door and started knocking. The kids began to stir and the cows began to get restless. The man realizes that he has two choices—give the guy what he wanted or lose a whole night's sleep to his persistence. He chose the former.

It is easy to misunderstand this parable. If the guy upstairs represents God, then God is reluctant to answer. Is Jesus teaching we must make ourselves a nuisance to browbeat the Almighty into giving us what we want? Many people never pray because this is how they view God—a reluctant neighbor who fights our requests even as He judges our failures. But breathe easy. The guy upstairs does not show us how God is, but how God is not. The key to this interpretation comes in verse 13 where Jesus concludes: "If you then, though you are evil, know how to give good gifts to your children, how much more will your Father in heaven give the Holy Spirit to those who ask Him!"

Jesus is not comparing God to the reluctant neighbor, but contrasting him to the reluctant neighbor. Jesus introduced him in verse 5, which can be translated, "Can any of you *even imagine* a friend doing this?" If a friend would not, surely the God of heaven would not! He is ever vigilant (He never sleeps nor slumbers), welcoming to all, and eager to help His children. Thus Jesus' message in the parable is clear: if a man's persistence gains him favor from a hard-hearted oaf who just wants to sleep, how much more favor will persistence gain from a generous heavenly Father who just wants to help?

We do not labor in prayer because we have to wear God down before He will answer. Yes, effective prayer demands persistence. But we persist, not with the heart of a prisoner manipulating a calloused guard, but of a child imploring a caring parent. That is the difference between persisting and pestering. Pestering assumes hostility, but persistence assumes

☼

When I met Christ, it seemed as though life were rather like a bike ride,

But it was a tandem bike, and I noticed that Christ was in the back helping me pedal.

I do not know just when it was that He suggested we change places,

But life has not been the same since . . . When He took the lead,

He knew delightful long cuts, up mountains and through rocky places

At breakneck speeds. It was all I could do to hang on!

Even though it looked like madness, He said, "Pedal!"

I worried and was anxious and asked, "Where are you taking me?"

He laughed and did not answer, and I started to learn to trust . . .

I did not trust Him, at first, in control of my life. I thought He'd wreck it;

But He knows bike secrets: how to make it take sharp corners,

How to jump to clear high rocks, How to fly to shorten scary passages.

And I am learning how to shut up and pedal in the strangest places,

And I'm beginning to enjoy the view and the cool breeze on my face . . .

(Author unknown)

love. God wants you to persist in prayer from hope in His love. Prayer is not prevailing over God's reluctance, but harnessing His willingness.

And how welcome is God's willingness to hear our prayers from the Valley! We are hurting people living in a world of hurt. We already had earthquakes, tornados, hurricanes, oil leaks, pollution, and politics. Sinners all from birth, we already had wars and hatred and greed and disease (and politics). And now, as if to add insult to injury, we have cancer! This is bad news, if not new news.

But cheer up! Jesus' good news for us as Valley dwellers is that yes, we are sin-sick people on a death-sentenced planet, but God has acted to heal us and it. He sent His Son Jesus to create a kingdom of redemption that will one day come to eternal fruition in a place called heaven where our bodies and our souls and our universe will be healed and made whole. And in the meantime on this death-sentenced planet, substantial healing is possible. In fact, we, God's people, are called to be agents of that healing through persistent prayer.

The great prayer warriors of history get it that we persist in prayer because of the promises of God. As Hudson Taylor wrote to his wife during an especially trying time in the work of the China Inland Mission over 150 years ago, "We have twenty-five cents—and all the promises of God!"[1]

Charles Spurgeon likened prayer to pulling a rope on earth that makes a great bell ring in the ears of God. "Some scarcely stir the bell. Others give but an occasional pluck at the rope, but he who wins with heaven is the man who grasps the rope boldly and pulls continuously, with all his might." Believing prayer pulls the rope continuously until God responds to the ringing! Do you offer your prayers in the faith that God hears, God cares, and ultimately, God will respond? And do you keep the bell ringing in heaven by praying persistently on earth?

As your Travel Writer, I feel confident that you will have a whole new level of interest in the power of healing prayer here in the Valley. When persistent, it is powerful.

The famous prayer warrior George Mueller summed up the importance of praying persistently when he said: "The great point is to never give up until the answer comes . . . the great fault of the children of God is: They do not continue in prayer; they do not go on praying; they do not persevere. If they desire anything for God's glory, they should pray until they get it." No, you do not have to butter up the Lord or wear Him down with a bunch of meaningless sweet nothings. Just love Him and persevere in prayer, and He will respond with His best for you.

2. Pray Patiently

> *So I say to you: Ask and it will be given to you; seek and you will find; knock and the door will be opened to you. (Luke 11:9)*

To pray persistently requires patience, and patience implies a relationship with God in which we are walking with Him, not just issuing orders to a short-order cook. The tense of the verbs in verse 9 reads, "*keep on* asking, *keep on* seeking, *keep on* knocking."

What is the one element that Christ wants with His people? Love. Do you think Jesus wants people terrified of Him and shrinking before Him, obeying His Word from expedience and not love? No way. As commendable as it is to take Jesus at His Word, that is not the ultimate destination of faith. It is not about doing *for* divine favors; it is about doing *from* divine love.

St. Augustine described the relational aspect of prayer in this short parable: "The man in the boat who throws a rope at a rock does not do it to pull the rock to the boat, but the boat to the rock. Christ is the rock, and we throw the rope through prayer." God does not want you to use your prayer time as the "favor of the day" moment only. He does not only want your requests, but your relationship as well. That means approaching Him in prayer as a means to relationship. That means hanging with God patiently as you pray.

The point of walking with God is not arriving, but walking with God. And the key to walking with God is patient prayer. "For everyone who asks receives; the one who seeks finds; and to the one who knocks, the door will be opened" (Luke 11:10).

Patience is required for effective prayer because all prayers are not equal. Some take more time, more effort, more wisdom to see accomplished than others. That seems to be the progression in "ask, seek, and knock." "Ask" prayers are simple requests with short-term life spans and tangible results. "Lord, lead me to the car I should buy." "Seek" prayers are deeper, harder, and slower. They involve us in more trial and testing and faith and discipline. We pray them wondering why God is dealing with us in a certain way. We do not know all the answers and that is why we become introspective as we listen for God's voice. "Seeking" in the Old Testament was often associated with repentance and self-examination.

"Knock" prayers are the hardest and most inward of all. The answers to such prayers come the slowest, test us the most, and yet turn out to be the greatest. Asking is request, seeking is urgency, and knocking? Well, that is desperation. Desperate prayers are the hardest because they require the most faith.

The following letter was found in a baking powder can wired to the handle of an old pump near a seldom-used trail across Nevada's Amargosa Desert:

> *This pump is all right as of June 1932. But the washer dries out and the pump has got to be primed. Under the white rock I buried a bottle of water, out of the sun and cork end up. There is enough water in it to prime the pump, but not if you drink some first. Pour about one-fourth and let her soak to wet the leather. Then pour in the rest medium fast and pump like crazy. You'll git water. The well has never run dry. Have faith. When you git watered up, fill the bottle and put it back like you found it for the next feller. (signed) Desert Pete.*
>
> *P.S. Do not go drinking the water first. Prime the pump with it and you'll git all you can hold.*

Our thirsty traveler in the desert story could see the water in the bottle, but he could only believe that water was actually in the well. He had to make a decision. Is seeing believing, or is believing seeing? He did not have the luxury of receiving and then believing. He had to believe first and only then receive. So must we sometimes, and that requires a mature faith! On the wall of a concentration camp a condemned prisoner once wrote: "I believe in the sun, even though it does not shine. I believe in love, even when it is not shown. I believe in God, even when He does not speak." "Knocking" prayers are prayers that stretch our faith even as they exercise our souls.

What is God's purpose in all of this? When we are asking, seeking, knocking, patiently and persistently walking through the ups and downs of life in relationship with God, is when God reaches us, teaches us, deepens us, and uses us. Without the harder, the easier would allow our hearts for Christ to grow cold. Oh, and it is also so that He can answer our prayers!

3. Pray Pliably

Last but not least, Jesus wants us to pray pliably. In a *Calvin and Hobbes* comic strip, it is late November and Calvin is waiting with his sled for the first big snowfall. He waits and waits, but no snow comes. He looks to heaven and says, "Okay, God, 1, 2, 3—ready, SNOW!" Nothing happens, and Calvin is upset. He shouts, "I said, Snow!" Nothing. He exclaims, "What is wrong with you God? Do you want me to become an atheist?"

Such petulance arises from the Jesus-as-ATM view of prayer. Not only does Calvin demand that God produce in response to his prayer, but it's got to be a specific response. He is not open and pliable to God's answering prayer according to His own love, wisdom, and plan. It must be snow, now, or else the highway for God!

Please notice that Jesus has nowhere promised that the persistent, patient pray-er gets *exactly* what they want. When they ask, they receive—but what? It is the same with seeking and knocking—God responds, but it may not be exactly in the way you had imagined. God is still good and has your interests at heart even if the answer He gives to you is not precisely what you had requested. Hear Jesus' words:

> *Which of you fathers, if your son asks for a fish, will give him a snake instead? Or if he asks for an egg, will give him a scorpion? (Luke 11:11–12)*

Now fish and eggs must have been hot items among the youth of Jesus' day! When sons asked their dads for these items, Jesus does not say they get them. He does say those fathers will be careful not to give their children that which would harm them—snakes and scorpions! No father would give his son a razor blade or loaded gun—no matter how politely he asked. No mom would let her daughter play in the medicine chest or around a hot burner—even if she asked. If we lovingly screen our children's requests, should not God have the same right? If human parents give their children what they know is best for them, cannot God be trusted to do the same for His?

St. Augustine once chased women and booze all over fourth-century northern Africa. But his Christian mother was a tenacious prayer warrior. When Augustine told her he was going to Rome, Monica prayed with all her heart that he would not go to the world's center of debauchery. But he went anyway and from there to Milan. God did not answer her prayer . . . exactly. In Milan, Augustine encountered Bishop Ambrose, who introduced him to Jesus Christ. He stopped chasing women and started pursuing the Lord instead. In later years, Augustine commented on his mother's prayer: "What she asked for was denied, but what she hoped for was granted."

Since the Lord is a good God who loves you, if He says no to you, it is only to say yes to something greater. As Jesus says, "If you . . . though you are evil, know how to give good gifts to your children, how much more will your Father in heaven give the Holy Spirit to those who ask him!" (Luke 11:13). The "Holy Spirit" here represents all the good things we will ever need for spiritual vitality. The parallel verse in Matthew 7:11

makes this clear: "If you then, though you are evil, know how to give good gifts to your children, how much more will your Father in heaven give good gifts to those who ask him!" As the Father's children, we must understand that God always answers our prayers in such a way that we receive good things, which are the best blessings God has to offer through the Holy Spirit— such as love, discernment, maturity, obedience, faith, power. If our prayers are pliable, we will gratefully receive what He gives even if it is not exactly what we requested.

The wisdom of pliable prayer can be seen in a note found on the body of a Confederate soldier.

> *I asked for strength that I might achieve. He made me weak that I might obey. I asked for health that I might do greater things. I was given grace that I might do better things. I asked for riches that I might be happy. I was given poverty that I might be wise. I asked for power that I might have the praise of men. I was given weakness that I might feel the need of God. I asked for all things that I might enjoy life. I was given life that I might enjoy all things. I received nothing that I asked for, all that I hoped for. My prayer was answered.*

Jesus illustrated this in John 4 when He refused the request of a nobleman of Herod Antipas's court who had made the eighteen-mile journey from Capernaum on a fast horse to breathlessly plead, "Jesus, you gotta come. He is dying. My boy, he is sick, bad sick. Please come and heal him!" He believed Jesus had to be there to physically touch and heal his son. He told Jesus what he wanted, and how Jesus ought to do it. "Come down." But what if Jesus did not want to come down? Did not need to come down? Do you ever presume to tell God how to do His job? When He does not make it happen the way you want, you assume He is not answering your prayer. Jesus intended to heal the boy, but He would do it in His own way. He told him, "Your son is living" and the man "took Jesus at his word and departed." He said, "Lord, you said it; that settles it; I believe it." Case closed.

Another key passage that illustrates the importance of praying pliable prayers is James 5, an extraordinary promise of healing in response to prayer that God makes through Jesus' half brother James:

> *Is anyone among you in trouble? Let them pray. Is anyone happy? Let them sing songs of praise. Is anyone among you sick? Let them call the elders of the church to pray over them and anoint them with oil in the name of the Lord. And the prayer offered in faith will make the sick person well; the Lord will raise them up. (Verses 13–15)*

What an amazingly precious and powerful promise of the power of prayer! And yet, the very power of the promise presents a problem to us here in the Valley, i.e., "the prayer offered in faith will make the sick person well," just does not square with our experience. After all, most of us have prayed for people who got worse instead of better.

If we are going to pray pliably as Jesus asks, we first need to understand what God's promise to heal does not mean: that a physical cure is always assured through the elders' prayer of faith or that sickness is caused by sin. Though we are free to ask Him, we have to accept that it is not always God's will to heal us physically.

If we are going to pray pliably, we also need to understand what these verses *do* mean. They do mean that spiritual and emotional healing is assured through the elders' prayer of faith, and that a physical cure may result as well if it is God's will. The word translated "restore" (NASB) or "make well" (NIV) in verse 15 is *sosei,* "will save." In the context of physical sickness, this word *can* refer to physical healing. But at a more profound level, it means spiritual restoration as it does in 1 Peter 2:24: "'He himself bore our sins' in his body on the cross, so that we might die to sins and live for righteousness; 'by his wounds you have been healed.'" Thus biblical healing for which God wants us to pray means more than just removing a disease, and "making us well" may include yet not even primarily encompass physical deliverance.

My friend Ray Pritchard puts it succinctly: "Healing in the Bible is not becoming what we were but becoming all that God intends us to be." It does not necessarily mean running the clock backwards so the accident never happened or the cancer never invaded. *Healing moves us forward.* We are "healed" as we come into right relationship with God, and that touches every part of us—yes body, but also and even primarily soul and spirit. We can easily feel defeated and hopeless and even bitter in times of sickness. In such times, we need to have our hope rejuvenated, our perspective restored, our sinful attitudes forgiven, and our focus sharpened. In my experience in praying for the sick and anointing with oil, this is what always happens. The sick person is "raised up" (15b) to new acceptance of God's will and trust in God's purpose and love for God's people. They are "saved" or "healed" of bitterness and faithlessness.

Finally, these verses do mean that God promises ultimate physical and spiritual healing in eternity through the prayer of faith. This is good news because, as important as physical healing is, we must remember that all healing in this life is partial and temporary. Of the forty-one people who experienced miracles of healing in the gospels, all died eventually. Even Lazarus whom Jesus raised from the dead (John 11) eventually died again. So when James declares, "The Lord *will* raise them up . . ." that is great news! And when that happens, we *will* be healed, period. That this *will* happen is the certainty of the gospel. No more sadness, pain, or tears. No more sin or death. Heaven, in short, in its marvelous magnitude and scope, constitutes the sure fulfillment of God's healing promise in response to the prayer of faith: Our bodies *will* be immortal, our souls *will* be restored, our spirits *will* be purified, our universe *will* be made whole. No doubt. No question. No worries.

I'm not suggesting that we should not pray for healing in the physical sense. We should, and we here in the Valley are intent on doing that daily! It is just that we are wise to be pliable when making that prayer, knowing that God may or may not choose to heal us sooner rather than later. I am thinking of my dad, Eric, who died last year. He had been ill for some time, and we were praying persistently for his healing.

☼

When my friend Kim was a young girl, her dad pulled the car off the road one day to help a woman change a flat tire. While he was lying under her car, another vehicle accidentally swerved to the shoulder, and in the collision the car was shoved onto his chest. His right thumb was torn off at the joint, five of his ribs were broken, and his left lung was pierced and began filling with blood. His wife, who is barely five feet tall, placed her hands on the bumper of the car and prayed, "In the name of the Lord Jesus Christ," and lifted the car off his chest so he could be dragged out. (Some weeks later she found out that she broke a vertebra in the effort.)

Kim's father was in a state of shock as he was taken to the hospital. Doctors prepared him for emergency surgery. "His thumb won't do him any good if he is dead," one of them said. His survival was iffy. Suddenly, spontaneously, the man's skin changed from ashen to pink. He experienced a miraculous healing. The surgical team did not even bother to hook him up to oxygen. He did not find out until later that this was the precise moment his father-in-law, who was a pastor, had his congregation start to pray for him.

Sometimes these stories come from not-very-credible sources—such as publications sold in grocery checkout lines that also carry news about extraterrestrial creatures secretly playing third base for the Boston Red Sox. In this case, however, the subject was James Loder, a professor at Princeton Theological Seminary. His life was not only saved, but changed. Until then, although he taught at a seminary, God had been mostly an abstract idea to him. Now Jesus became a living Presence. Kim writes that her father's heart grew so tender that he became known at Princeton as "the weeping professor." He began to live from one moment to the next in a God-bathed, God-soaked, God-intoxicated world.[2]

According to James, those prayers were right! But even as we prayed, we knew we were like children looking through a keyhole. We see so little. God sees so much. We see a part. God sees the whole. And in His seeing, the Lord chose not to heal my dad physically in this world. But our family did not take this as unanswered prayer because we understand from Scripture that ultimate healing will not come until the dead in Christ are raised when Jesus comes again.[3] We are grateful for the biblical truth that salvation includes the redemption of the body, not just the redemption of the soul in heaven.[4] And so we were pliable in our prayers and therefore grateful to God when, instead of healing Dad in this life, He took him home where we know he is now healed physically and every other way that matters in heaven. No, I will not be satisfied until I see my dad once again, hear his hearty laugh, and feel him put his arm on my shoulder and say, with his Irish brogue, "Och Andy, how are you doing?" Memories are sweet, but nothing can take the place of seeing our loved ones once again. The beauty of God's healing promise is, we know we will. This then is the Faith Healer's credo: God does His healing work throughout eternity. And to that end we persist in prayer.

And so we find prayer powerful because through it, God always heals and sometimes miraculously heals. How, then, do we here in the Valley pray for the sick?[5]

We pray . . .

Aggressively, because nothing is impossible with God.

Fervently, because the prayers of the righteous are powerful and effective.[6]

Unitedly, because our faith grows stronger as we pray together.

Trustingly, knowing that we have a High Priest who invites us to come to the throne of grace where we can find grace and mercy in the time of need.

Repeatedly, because God invites us to ask, ask, and keep on asking.

Confidently, knowing that the Lord will not turn us away when we call out to Him.

Gratefully, because we have already received "grace upon grace," far more than we deserve.

Submissively, because God's understanding of the total situation is much greater than ours. That way we can wholeheartedly accept God's answers to our prayers no matter what they are.

Tony Campolo tells about preaching in a church and later being asked to pray for healing for a man there who had cancer. That next week he got a call from the man's wife. "You prayed for my husband. He died." Campolo's heart sank until she added, "But it is okay. When he came to church that Sunday he was fifty-eight and angry that all-powerful God did not cure his cancer. He would lie in bed and curse God and sometimes everybody around him. But after you prayed for him, he found peace. The last three days have been the best days of our lives. We've sung. We've laughed. We've read Scripture. We prayed. Thank you for praying for him. He was not cured, but Tony, he was healed."

So God calls His people to pray in the Valley. And here is how. Pray persistently; it is always too soon to give up. Pray patiently; develop your relationship with God while seeking and knocking and asking. And pray pliably; submit your will to God's will, honor Him as the Lord, and trust Him to answer your prayers wisely and well. If we do our part, God will never fail to do His. Never.

Your Pedaling in the
Strangest Places Travel
Writer,

Pastor Andy

4

STARS: THE BEAUTY OF SUFFERING

☼

SEVERAL YEARS AGO, MY THREE-YEAR-OLD NEPHEW AND I WERE STANDING IN FRONT OF A LARGE WINDOW, WATCHING IT RAIN. HE STARTED SAYING, "STARS, STARS, STARS." I TURNED TO MY SISTER-IN-LAW AND ASKED, "WHY DOES HE KEEP REPEATING STARS, STARS, STARS?" SHE ANSWERED, "HE THINKS THAT WHEN RAINDROPS HIT THE GROUND, FOR A SPLIT SECOND THEY LOOK LIKE STARS."[1]

Dear Fellow Travelers,

Suffering is a staple of travel here in the Valley as you no doubt have discovered, or soon will. As your Travel Writer, one of the more counterintuitive truths I am keen for you to grasp is that, though the suffering that comes with cancer is ugly, its effects in and through you can be beautiful if you place it in God's hands. Virtually everyone here is acquainted with the ugly. But I am jealous for you to behold the beautiful.

I did not do this when I first entered the Valley. I was too preoccupied with the suffering to see anything good in it. Ever since I saw *Braveheart* I had wondered what it would be like to meet up with the business end of a sword. What with two major surgeries literally under my belt, I now know. The first one produced a three-inch incision plus three puncture wounds, and the second one a seven-inch incision in my abdomen that took thirty-two staples to close. I do admit Mel Gibson's character probably had it much worse what with no general anesthesia or Vicodin (my new best friend), but still . . . I'd never experienced such exquisite pain.

After both surgeries it (really!) hurt to cough, laugh, stand up, sit down, walk, turn over in bed, scratch, stretch, or even yell at politicians on TV. Other than that, it was a breeze. I even got a new nickname from my staff at church after losing twelve inches of my colon: "Semicolon." Now my friends call me "Semi-C" for short. Lovely.

Little did I know that surgery for me was merely practice for the big game—eighteen months of chemotherapy. My chemo adventure also began with minor surgery to install a handy dandy portacath right under my left clavicle. I was grateful for this ingenious device because it spared me the deleterious assault on my veins that the biweekly infusion of the FOLFOX regimen chemo drugs would have exacted, though to my consternation I soon learned it sat right under my car seat belt where it rubbed incessantly for nearly two years.

Three drugs make up this delightful FOLFOX concoction: leucovorin, fluorouracil, and my favorite, oxaliplatin, which makes your tissues, especially in hands and throat, hypersensitive to cold. For months, I had to get cold packages out of the fridge with gloves and could drink nothing cold . . . no ice in Texas in summertime! But that was a mild inconvenience compared to the coming flurry of unpleasantness.

FOLFOX has a cornucopia of side effects: fatigue, hair thinning (if not total loss), nausea, intestinal problems (read: gnarly constipation), sore gums and throat, skin and nail problems, neuropathy and muscle problems, eye and vision and blood count changes. They also produce chemo brain—not a desirable trait—but a mental fog that extinguishes memory, concentration, multitasking, and use of the English language. It rendered me slightly more advanced than a mollusk on the Atlantic floor (and, as my wife will attest, this condition never quite goes away).

FOLFOX gifted me with bowel movements like volcanic magma singeing its way through my system, leaving flaming skin irritation and a crying need for a dubiously named product called (I kid you not) "Butt Paste."[2] And it also multiplied mouth sores so bad that I went days without being able to speak and on occasion had to use baby-teething gum anesthetics on the inside of my cheeks to be able to preach at church.

None of these undesirable effects are surprising when you consider that, when a chemo bag breaks in the lab, they get guys in Hazmat suits to clean it up. This is virulent poison they're pumping into your body, hoping to kill cancer cells just before they kill you. These treatments have proven to be not just miserable and painful but boring as well, rather like getting a root canal spaced out over eighteen months of watching old *Lawrence Welk* reruns—sharp discomfort punctuated by multiple seasons of aimlessness, fatigue, nearly constant nausea, and overall blah. I feel like the small boy I once was, forced to wonder through interminable adult worship services in my dad's Presbyterian church: "Will this *ever* end?"

That is the question about suffering that first preoccupied me in the Valley. I just wanted the pain and misery to end. I was not interested in exploring how God might use these in and through my life to produce something beautiful. But unfortunately, wishing pain away does not actually make it go away, and with that option gone, I began to perk up and listen to other strategies for dealing with suffering such as that of St. Francis de Sales, a Catholic missionary who lived from 1567–1622.

> *Be at peace. Do not look forward in fear to the changes in life; but rather, to them with full hope as they arise. God, whose very own you are, will deliver you from out of them. He has kept you hitherto, and He will lead you safely through all things; and when you cannot stand it, God will bury you in His arms. Do not fear what may happen tomorrow; the same everlasting Father who cares for you today will take care of you then and every day. He will either shield you from suffering*

☼

Billy Graham tells the story of a friend who lost it all: his job, fortune, family, future. The only thing he had left was his faith in God. One day he stopped to watch some workmen repairing the spire of a great cathedral in his city. A stonemason chipping away at a tiny triangular piece of stone grabbed his attention. He asked the man what he was doing. The worker motioned to the spire and said, "Look all the way to the top." When the man did, he saw a tiny triangular space near the peak of the spire. The worker said, "I'm shaping this down here so it will fit up there." That's precisely what God is doing through His gift of purpose in suffering; He's shaping us down here so that we will fit up there. He is building godly character in us through the only strategy sufficient to the task: suffering.

or will give you unfailing strength to bear it. Be at peace and put aside all anxious thoughts and imaginations.

St. Francis found peace even in the prospect of suffering because he had hope from God for ultimate deliverance. He believed that suffering is not an aberration in the lives of God's children, but a purposeful part of God's plan to produce beauty in and through us as He personally leads us through this Valley. Ray Pritchard expressed in a sermon the same hope in terms of the providence of God: "God's providence means that . . . nothing is wasted in a believer's life. Even the things that seem to be setbacks, roadblocks, and defeats—even those things are not wasted by God. He never allows anything to happen in your life by chance. Everything—even those things that seem like mistakes—has a divinely ordered purpose."

Because suffering therefore is not just ugly, but purposeful, we children of God can endure it with peace and "put aside all anxious thoughts and imaginations," not by resenting it in bitterness, but by embracing it in faith. People here have learned to do that by focusing on the beautiful, purposeful things God wants to do in and through us through suffering. As your Travel Writer, I encourage you to acknowledge these beautiful by-products of suffering as soon as possible. If you do, they will make your trip instantly better.

SUFFERING AND CHARACTER

Paul was no stranger to suffering. Here's what he had to say about the beauty it produces: "Not only so, but we also glory in our sufferings, because we know that suffering produces perseverance; perseverance, character; and character, hope. And hope does not disappoint us, because God's love has been poured out into our hearts through the Holy Spirit, who has been given to us" (Romans 5:3–5).

Paul says we rejoice in the midst of suffering because it produces perseverance, which produces character. Character is the blockbuster term here. In Greek it is *dokimos* and means "passed the test." In the ancient world, if a potter put a vessel in the furnace and it didn't crack, on the bottom he stamped "DIKIMOS," "approved."[3] This is a vessel of character. It has withstood the test of fire. It has been refined. It hasn't broken. It is whole and complete, just what God wants in the character of His beloved ones.

That is what God says suffering does if we allow it to refine our character. However, we can instead just lie back and allow it to embitter our hearts instead. Suffering in and of itself automatically makes us miserable, but not good. If we do not trust God by embracing suffering to refine our character, then suffering will leave us who we were, only more miserable. But if we allow and implore Him to do so, God uses suffering (the Greek word is *thlipsis,* meaning "to be pressed down") to wake us up to our weakness and His strength and to deepen our ability to persevere (the Greek word means to bear up under) without giving up. Suffering makes those who feel invincible, vulnerable; those who pride themselves on being independent, dependent; the insensitive more sensitive; the arrogant humble; and the tough tenderized.

It is no accident that Jesus Christ, the God-Man Himself, was approved for ministry through the molding of misery. Right after His temptation ordeal in the wilderness, He went into Galilee preaching, teaching, and healing. By God's design, His suffering outfitted Him for this ministry. The writer of Hebrews put it this way: "Since he himself has gone through suffering and testing, he is able to help us when we are being tested" (Hebrews 2:18 NLT). Jesus took no shortcuts to character significance, and neither must we since God's desire is that we become just like His Son:

> *And we know that in all things God works for the good of those who love him, who have been called according to his purpose. For those God foreknew he also predestined to be conformed to the image of his Son, that he might be the firstborn among many brothers and sisters. And*

During World War II, a decorated young Russian captain was arrested for criticizing Joseph Stalin. He spent eight years in prison and decades of exile from his homeland. He was Alexander Solzhenitsyn, one of the most influential writers of the twentieth century. No stranger to suffering, Solzhenitsyn penned the *Gulag Archipelago*, a Nobel Prize–winner that brought the ravages of Soviet communism to world attention. Solzhenitsyn believed that his unjust ordeal in prison was in truth God's preparation for his life's work: "Formerly you never forgave anyone. You judged people without mercy. And you praised people with equal lack of moderation. And now an understanding mildness has become the basis of your uncategorical judgments. You have come to realize your own weaknesses—and you can therefore understand the weaknesses of others. Your soul, which formerly was dry, now ripens from suffering."[4]

those he predestined, he also called; those he called, he also justified; those he justified, he also glorified. (Romans 8:28–30)

God chose us to become like His Son. To that end, He uses everything and wastes nothing. He cares about the tiniest details of our lives. With God there is no big or small. He knows when a sparrow falls and He numbers the hairs on your head. He keeps track of the stars in the skies and the rivers that flow to the oceans. He sets the day of your birth and death and ordains everything that comes to pass in between. What an encouraging reassurance: there are no accidents with God, only incidents that prove that God is looking out for you.

The result of our suffering in this Valley can be beautiful because, if you allow it, it produces godly character. So please, my friends, allow it. As Rob Bell says, "We are going to suffer, and it is going to shape us. Somehow. We will become bitter or better, closed or open, more ignorant or more aware, more or less tuned in to the thousands upon thousands of gifts we are surrounded with every single moment of every single day. This too will shape me."[5]

SUFFERING AND MINISTRY

We here in the Valley have also come to appreciate another beautiful thing that God brings through suffering that is offered to Him: redemption. This is a great mystery to us, but we know it is true. Resented suffering is destructive. But redeemed suffering is redemptive. When by faith we offer our suffering to God, He redeems it and makes it redemptive. When we choose joy in the midst of our suffering and pain, God does a very special thing. He makes our suffering into a royal sacrifice that has great value. It mysteriously yet powerfully contributes to Christ's finished act of redemption on the cross. Our suffering becomes one with His. That's how Paul viewed his own suffering.

Now I rejoice in what I am suffering for you, and I fill up in my flesh what is still lacking in regard to Christ's afflictions, for the sake

> *of his body, which is the church. I have become its servant by the commission God gave me to present to you the word of God in its fullness—the mystery that has been kept hidden for ages and generations, but is now disclosed to the Lord's people. To them God has chosen to make known among the Gentiles the glorious riches of this mystery, which is Christ in you, the hope of glory. (Colossians 1:24–27).*

Far be it from us who suffer in this Valley to assume that our pain is somehow necessary to complete the redemptive sufferings of Christ on the cross. Yet there does seem to be a mysterious sense in which God gifts us who suffer with the gratification of knowing that, in some wonderful exchange, our offered suffering is counted in the win column for the redemption of the world.

Paul had a noble mission in life that made his life significant no matter how much he suffered. He was about the business of sharing the truth of Christ and building up the body of Christ no matter what it cost him. John Piper writes, "Christ's cross was for propitiation; ours is for propagation. Christ suffered to accomplish salvation. We suffer to spread salvation."[6] Since the church is Christ's body, when Paul who was part of the church suffered, Christ suffered. What Jesus began as suffering with His persecution and rejection on earth, believers complete in His continuing body on earth.

When we Christ-followers bear up under suffering out of conscience toward God and all that He is doing in and through our distress, we become conduits to an unbelieving world of the indisputable truth of Christ in them, the hope of glory. Our suffering, properly understood and faithfully offered to God, becomes the occasion for people far from God to be confronted with the hope of the gospel. Our suffering thus joins with Christ's redemptive suffering to redeem the lost. It's that reality that helps us suffering Christians persevere, because we are blessed in knowing that our suffering is never in vain.

As I noted above, this connection between our suffering and God's redemptive work in the world is a great gift to us here in the Valley because it affords us a way to put our suffering to work for good. It is no longer merely pain to be endured, but an opportunity to be exploited. It is no longer merely misery experienced in isolation, but ministry practiced in collaboration. And it has a powerful effect on those around us.

My chemo infusions are biweekly and punctuated with an electronic pump that continues to pump chemo into my portacath for an extra forty-eight hours after I leave the lab. I have learned to dread the periodic cycling of that pump, which I can hear and even feel as the poison swaggers into my bloodstream, stirring up waves of nausea. A common picture these days is of me sitting on the couch watching TV with the family, the chemo pump going, and me groaning all the way through *Masterpiece Theatre.* Funny, I find that making an audible expression of misery actually mitigates the pain. So the pump cycles and I groan and the world keeps turning. So has it always been in the Valley.

But God's grace allows me to accomplish more than just groaning in my suffering. Recognizing that this pain is no mistake and that God is with me, I am empowered to offer my suffering as a sacrifice to the Lord.

So I use my misery to prompt my prayer that God's trademark pattern will hold true—down to go up, life from death, beauty from ugliness. I ask and I believe that as I suffer disease and loss, good will come from it and that the good will be larger than the suffering it thereby redeems. I pray that my pain will not be in vain, but that somehow it will work with Christ's pain in the redemption of the world. The transformation of a suffering that distresses us to no end into an offering that glorifies God without end is an amazing gift that I pray you experience very soon.

SUFFERING AND GLORY

In and of itself, suffering is a gnarly, unattractive business. But dedicated to God, it produces good and beautiful things like godly character and redemptive ministry in and through God's children. It also leads to

☼

THOMAS LYNCH SAYS,

My mother's was a voice crying in the suburban wilderness that we were all given crosses to bear—it was our imitation of Christ—and we should offer it up for the suffering souls. That is how she turned it into prayer—the "irregularity," the cancer, the tumor . . . my mother was making it work for her, placing the pain and the fear and the grief of it into that account with God she'd kept, by which what was happening to her body became only one of several things that was happening to her. Her body, painful and tumorous, was turning on her and she was dying. I'm sure she was ready to be rid of it. She said her heart was overwhelmed with grief and excitement. Grief at the going from us . . . excitement at the going "home." She could see things none of us could see. She refused the morphine and remained lucid and visionary. She spoke words of comfort to each of us—at one point saying we must learn to let go, not only grudgingly, but as an act of praise. I say this not only because I understand it but because I witnessed it.[7]

beauty. "Amazing as the greatest of all gifts is, God the Son does more than save sinners. Jesus' life and death also change the character of suffering, give it dignity and weight and even, sometimes, a measure of beauty. Cancer and chronic pain remain ugly things, but the enterprise of living with them is not an ugly thing. God's Son so decreed it when he gave himself up to torture and death."[8]

As Jesus' submission to suffering ultimately led to glory, so it does for us as well. Paul says that if we trust God with our suffering, we get to share in Christ's glory.

> *Now if we are children, then we are heirs—heirs of God and co-heirs with Christ, if indeed we share in his sufferings in order that we may also share in his glory. I consider that our present sufferings are not worth comparing with the glory that will be revealed in us. For the creation waits in eager expectation for the children of God to be revealed. For the creation was subjected to frustration, not by its own choice, but by the will of the one who subjected it, in hope that the creation itself will be liberated from its bondage to decay and brought into the freedom and glory of the children of God. (Romans 8:17–21)*

The beauty of suffering in God's plan is not just that it produces people of character and faith, but also that it leads to glory for those people of character and faith.

In other words, our anxious longing in suffering and eager waiting in spite of pain is not asking too much. Heaven is worth the wait. So writes the apostle Peter:

> *God is keeping careful watch over us and the future. The Day is coming when you'll have it all—life healed and whole. I know how great this makes you feel, even though you have to put up with every kind of aggravation in the meantime. Pure gold put in the fire comes out of it proved pure; genuine faith put through this suffering comes out proved genuine. When Jesus wraps this all up, it's your*

☼

We have two fellow Valley-dwellers, my friends Jay and Beth, who are exercising that discipline magnificently and thus showing many of us the way forward to glory through suffering. Here is their most recent update on Jay's battle with cancer and its aftermath:

"Jay is still cancer-free and we continue to be so grateful for that. Most of the hardships have come from the high-dose steroids Jay took while surviving that life-threatening graft vs. host disease (GVHD) last summer. However, we're now suffering the dark side of those steroids. For example, as he began his conditioning last fall, we had no idea the steroids had left him with severe osteoporosis. Later, it caused six vertebra fractures and two cracked ribs. Within weeks, he had contracted the following lifelong conditions: hunched back, diabetes, cataracts, glaucoma, and neuropathy.

He has endured high doses of narcotics for pain, six back procedures, as well as ongoing symptoms of mild GVHD: loss of appetite, dry eyes/mouth, and constant nausea. What's particularly difficult is the belief that Jay was just weeks from the finish line last fall. All was fine, and then we experienced a cascade of serious issues—all side effects from steroid treatment necessary to save his life last year.

Jay has been in almost constant pain since February. Frankly, we are facing a level of chronic suffering we certainly did not anticipate. However, there is greater and unlimited truth in God's character of love and provision for us. We continue to see, daily, demonstrations of His love, care, and faithfulness to us. And so we are encouraged, as Paul said, to 'walk by faith, not by sight.' As always, thank you for walking with us."

Beth and Jay

faith, not your gold, that God will have on display as evidence of his victory. (1 Peter 1:5–7 MSG)

Faith on display in the midst of suffering is a powerful sign that the victorious kingdom of God is at hand. But such faith requires discipline. It requires choosing for the light even when there is much darkness to frighten us, choosing for life even when the forces of death are so visible, and choosing for the truth even when we are surrounded with lies. It requires suffering with perseverance, faith, love, and hope.

Even as my heart sinks in reading (see previous page) about Jay's incessant suffering, I am inspired by his and Beth's constancy of faith under fire. In this Valley, they are beautiful to me and the hundreds who know them and are praying for them. Their patience is extraordinary, their courage magnificent, and their fortitude unwavering. Because they are allowing God to use suffering to produce beauty in and through them, the hardship and pain they are undergoing are like those special raindrops that flash like stars in the split second that they touch down. Jay and Beth are stars to me and to all who know them and I am sure to God as well. Their faith through these terrible times has covered them in glory even as they offer all the glory to God. And the story God is telling in their lives goes on. I watch with admiration and bated breath to see what happens next.

Suffering is not a beautiful thing. But by the grace of God in the lives of His faithful children, it produces beautiful things. I don't like it, would never seek it, don't recommend it. But I appreciate what God does with it when I give it to Him. No one wants to suffer or to see their loved ones suffer, yet it's a staple here in the Valley. So we've learned not to flee it or resent it, but use it as a stage where grace exhibits God's glory.

People frequently ask me how I'm feeling in these days and I truthfully respond "pretty good." I am looking at things these days through very grateful eyes. I'm grateful to God for each new suffering-laden day to which I awaken. His grace and goodness is everywhere. It always was and will be, it's just that I'm seeing it more clearly now. And the only reason that's true is my suffering. It has become to me a conduit to character, a mode of ministry, and a gift of glory. I pray that the same will be true for you.

Your "Drops Like Stars"
Travel Writer,

Pastor Andy

5

HOMECOMING: THE GOODNESS OF GOD

IF YOU ATTEMPT TO TALK WITH A DYING MAN ABOUT SPORTS OR BUSINESS, HE IS NO LONGER INTERESTED. HE NOW SEES OTHER THINGS AS MORE IMPORTANT. PEOPLE WHO ARE DYING RECOGNIZE WHAT WE OFTEN FORGET, THAT WE ARE STANDING ON THE BRINK OF ANOTHER WORLD.[1]

My Dear Fellow Travelers,

It takes awhile to accept our appointment to our very special C club, because that means getting acclimated to the idea that this journey in the Valley could be our very last.

That is no easy process for any of us. Cancer kills a lot of people and we have cancer. Ergo, cancer may kill a lot of us. Barring God's miraculous intervention, I most likely have drawn one of the short sticks. My diagnosis is Stage IV colon cancer and my survival chances are 8 percent. I know, I know, 8 percent is not chopped liver. But it is a 92 percent supermajority vote for me to get my affairs in order. In my first meeting with Dr. Gerald Edelman, my oncologist and friend, his words were not about cure but "management." All of us in the Valley know that as a euphemism for making people as comfortable as possible while they die. So I'm going with the 92 percent and getting my affairs in order. Since you are in the Valley, you're welcome to tag along with me if you like.

As your faithful Travel Writer, I'm not going to beat around the bush. Death is the backdrop of this Valley of the Shadow. If you want a good visit here, you have to get your eyes wide open.

When I first got here, my daughter Julie Rhodes wrote this post, "Walking with Collin," on her blog for the Fort Worth Star-Telegram.

This week, my dad was diagnosed with colon cancer. Dad has taken to calling his condition "Collin Cancer," as if he and it are on a first-name basis. (My mother is quick to correct him.) My son Drew (21 months old), of course, has no concept or precedent for understanding that his grandfather is sick. He calls my dad "Pops." When we visit Pops at church (my dad is a pastor), Drew bursts into his office enthusiastically and immediately asks where his grandmother is. "Honey?" he says (Honey is her grandmother name). My mom is, of course, at home or somewhere else. Visiting Pops at church is very regimented, you see. This happens every time. And after the introductions have been made, Drew heads straight for Dad's golf balls and putter. Drew loves to roll the balls all around the office, usually losing two or three behind pieces of furniture.

Then I look at Drew and think a thought that astonishes even myself: Will I live to see the day he is diagnosed with colon cancer? Up to this week, the closest I have come to comprehending Drew's mortality is his recent habit of yelling, "Die!" in public places. He does this because he is now obsessed with the Music Man soundtrack—which is because I have been obsessed with it since my church is putting it on in September and I am learning my part. I play the CD in the car and Drew won't listen to anything else. One of the songs ends in the highest of high notes as Marian the Librarian sings the phrase, "him I could love 'til I die. Til I DIE!" Drew loves that last note and the purity of a one-syllable word he is able to pronounce. So we'll be at Target and some drivel will be playing over the sound system and Drew will demand petulantly, "die? Die? DIE?" "No die," I tell him, shushing him. I hope people around me don't interpret him to be telling me to drop dead, but that is a distinct possibility. But we will someday, won't we? I try not to let that thought cement me where I stand. I must keep walking. Dorothy Bernard has said, "Courage is fear that has said its prayers." I for one know Pops has said his prayers, and now it is time to say my own—for him, for Drew, and for myself.[2]

This is, I feel, the first order of business for everyone who visits the Valley of the Shadow of Death. . . . die? Die? DIE?" You've got to deal with death. Not death in the abstract. Not death as a philosophical construct or a sterile scientific reality. But death in the concrete. Specific death. Your own death. Possibly for the first time in your life, you're facing the likelihood that you may soon be shuffling off this mortal coil. We all knew that at some point we had to meet our Maker. *Incerta omnia, sola mors certa.* Of all things in the world, only death is not uncertain (and, of course, taxes, but we're taking one scourge at a time here). I hope this doesn't strike you as overly pessimistic but simply realistic. Cancer has a way of hastening meetings with our Maker, and the last thing we want is to be caught off guard.

Of course I recognize that even though you have entered the Valley, you may yet leave it for Myopia. You may receive healing, a cure may appear, and you may not complete your journey all the way through . . . this time. I hope and I pray that is the case, that you get well and that this little detour in the Valley was just an adventurous diversion and not a destination for you.

But if that healing does not come, what then? Nobody joins the cancer club of their own volition. People in the Valley realize this is a gig they get picked for, so even though they don't like it, they determine not to waste energy griping about how they don't want to be here. Rather, they work on how to traverse this desert joyfully, courageously, and faithfully even if the trip is a swan song, not a victory dance.

Just months before his own crossing over, a young pastor named

James van Tholen explained his cancer perspective to his congregation in his first sermon to them after seven months of surgery and chemotherapy.

> *We can't ignore what has happened. We can rise above it; we can live through it; but we can't ignore it. If we ignore the threat of death as too terrible to talk about, then the threat wins. Then we are overwhelmed by it, and our faith doesn't apply to it. And if that happens, we lose hope. We want to worship God in this church, and for our worship to be real, it doesn't have to be fun, and it doesn't have to be guilt-ridden. But it does have to be honest, and it does have to hope in God. We have to be honest about a world of violence and pain, a world that scorns faith and smashes hope and rebuts love. We have to be honest about the world, and honest about the difficulties of faith within it. And then we still have to hope in God.*[3]

James was right. It is sheer foolishness to blow smoke and obfuscate the unwelcome reality that many of us are dying right now. True hope can only be found if we gulp hard and swallow the honesty pill. Then things can get better. Then we can actually get good with dying. I mean that in the sense that a Texas ranch family gets good with tornadoes by building a storm shelter. They're still not enamored of twisters, but by God they are ready if one shows up. By God we can, and should, and must get good with death. As Richard John Neuhaus says in the opening sentence of his *As I Lay Dying*, "We are born to die. Not that death is the purpose of our being born, but we are born toward death, and in each of our lives the work of dying is already under way. The work of dying well is, in largest part, the work of living well."[4]

It seems ironic to us in the Valley that so many people only begin to think about their mortality when their life is almost over. In contrast, we have learned to admire the wisdom of those who, in St. Augustine's phrase, live their days "deafened by the clanking chains of mortality."

By living daily in the shadow of death, we discover as people of faith that death is but a shadow.

For me, getting good with dying first involved some long nights of the soul spent staring at the dark ceiling wondering what it was going to be like to die and getting aggravated because I had too much stuff still left to do. Former TV news anchor Tony Snow accurately describes my experience. "The mere thought of dying can send adrenaline flooding through your system. A dizzy, unfocused panic seizes you. Your heart thumps; your head swims. You think of nothingness and swoon. You fear partings; you worry about the impact on family and friends. You fidget and get nowhere."[5]

Along with those long nights, getting good with dying entailed completing some important practical projects. I spent days getting my life insurance in order, planning my own funeral (I have a file folder now with music, speaker, Scriptures, slide show ideas . . . it's going to be a lively affair!), and having the remarriage talk with my dear Alice.

But the most important element for me in getting good with dying was sweating the question that kept poking me in the eye every time I tried to pray. "Is God *really* good?"

I know that's a rather brash and even narcissistic query coming from a mere mortal just because he's got cancer. Essentially, the question is this: "How can God be good and let *me* die?" This isn't death in the abstract. What greater good do I have in my life than my very life? And if that's my greatest good, how can God be good if He lets cancer take it away from me? What an affront! The bewilderment we all face as people of faith in the face of our own impending death makes our hearts yearn for an explanation, a rationale, an apologetic which will address the seeming disconnect between God's love and our death. We just want to know, can we still believe God is good even though we die? Valley people are quite at peace in answering that question with a resounding yes. They possess the advantage of time spent in this anteroom to death that has given them a perspective on human mortality that most in the land of Myopia have never attained.

Even though entering the Valley at first feels like an insult from an uncaring God, the people here have gotten past taking it personally. So should you. After all, death has always been inevitable for everyone, even the young and healthy among us. In the Valley, it's just become imminent. "How is your wife?" the man asked a friend he had not seen for years. "She's in heaven." "Oh, I'm sorry!" he exclaimed. Then he quickly clarified, "I mean, I'm glad." That was even worse so he finally offered, "Well, I'm surprised!" Valley people are no longer surprised by death. Rather, they have defanged its fear and dispelled its mystery and, as a result, gotten good with death by reaffirming their faith in God's goodness. It's wise for all of us to do this whether we've entered the Valley or not. As Morrie Schwartz observes: "Everyone knows they're going to die . . . but nobody believes it. If we did, we would do things differently . . . There's a better approach. To know you're going to die, and to be prepared for it at any time. That's better. That way you can actually be more involved in your life while you're living."[6]

Morrie is right. When we allow the fear of death to make us avoid considering life's most important realities, we give it inordinate power over us. But preparation gives us power over it.

So how do we prepare? It's simple, really. By affirming and living out our faith in Christianity and the promises in God's Word. Faith is the only antidote to fear that I've discovered in thirty-five years of ministry. It is the only advocate that people here in the Valley have when fighting the fear of death in their soul's dark nights.

For years it was my privilege to be one of those clergy who affirmed that to be absent from the body is to be present with the Lord (2 Corinthians 5:8). Now it's my turn to be on the receiving end of that message. Without faith in that mystery, we are cast adrift in terrifying unknowns. What happens to us when we die? Are we conscious? Do we go through a tunnel of light? Is death like an eternal nap from which

☼

When . . . we remain unprepared for the Ultimatum certainly to seize us, then the death that interrupts our daily lives is monstrous. Fight against it with all your might. Hate it. Be filled with envy and anger for those who are still healthy. Wail, plead, beg, make deals with friends and with the Infinite. Sink into despair. Lie down in hopelessness. Die, then—even before you die. Or else, prepare. Long before that final confrontation, prepare.[7]

we never awaken? Is there a heaven and hell, a heaven and no hell, a hell and no heaven? Can I know which is my future address? No wonder W. C. Fields had these words chiseled on his tombstone: "I'd rather be in Philadelphia," and Woody Allen admitted, "It's not that I'm afraid to die. I just don't want to be there when it happens." The uncertainties of death make it fearful, a proud and powerful enemy. It frightens us because it mystifies us.

I love what funeral director and poet Thomas Lynch says:

> *The afterlife seems to make the most sense after life—when someone we love is dead on the premises. The bon vivant abob in his hot tub needs heaven like another belly button. Faith is for the heartbroken, the embittered, the doubting, and the dead. And funerals are the venues at which such folks gather. Some among the clergy have learned to like it. Thus they present themselves at funerals with a good cheer and an unambiguous sympathy that would seem like duplicity in anyone other than a person of faith. I count among the great blessings of my calling that I have known men and women of such bold faith, such powerful witness, that they stand between the dead and the living and say, "Behold I tell you a mystery."*[8]

But God's Word enables us to see death from a new perspective that frees us from the fear of death. It records the story of God's wonderful intervention in mankind's rush to self-destruction when our forebears rebelled against God and set the forces of death into motion. Death was never God's intention for human beings. It is unnatural, intrusive, and evil. But when Adam chose to serve sin instead of God, he brought death upon the human race. The fear of death and its condemnation held people prisoner from the beginning. It made us slaves. But Jesus Christ, God's Son, entered our world to die that we might live. He is God's Great Emancipator: ". . . It has now been revealed through the appearing of our Savior, Christ Jesus, who has destroyed death and has brought life and immortality to light through the gospel" (2 Timothy 1:10). This promise fueled John Donne, eighteenth-century poet and Anglican priest, to write a famous rebuke of death during London's bubonic plague even as he thought himself fatally infected:

Death be not proud, though some have called thee
Mighty and dreadfull, for thou art not so . . .
One short sleepe past, wee wake eternally
And death shall be no more; death, thou shalt die.

So it shall! As a result of Jesus' atoning work in our place on the cross, we have faith that death is no longer master over us. His death killed death for us, so that now instead of a destiny, death is a passageway to an even better life. So says God. "Since the children have flesh and blood, he too shared in their humanity so that by his death he might break the power of him who holds the power of death—that is, the devil—and free those who all their lives were held in slavery by their fear of death" (Hebrews 2:14–15).

In *Facing Death and the Life After,* Billy Graham relates an experience of Donald Grey Barnhouse, one of America's leading Bible teachers in the first half of the twentieth century. Cancer took Dr. Barnhouse's first wife, leaving him with three children all under the age of twelve. The day of the funeral, Barnhouse and his family were driving to the service when a large truck passed them, casting a noticeable shadow across their car. Turning to his oldest daughter who was staring sadly out the window, Barnhouse asked, "Tell me, sweetheart, would you rather be run over by that truck or its shadow?" Looking curiously at her father, she replied, "By the shadow, I guess. It can't hurt you." Speaking to all his children, he then said, "Your mother has not been overridden by death, but by the shadow of death. That is nothing to fear."

Christians in the Valley of the Shadow of Death need not fear dying, because they know shadows can't hurt them. Rather for the believer, death is the last shadow before heaven's dawn. The fundamental hope of Christ-followers with respect to death is, therefore, resurrection. As

Paul writes, "Indeed, we felt we had received the sentence of death. But this happened that we might not rely on ourselves but on God, who raises the dead" (2 Corinthians 1:9). Faith gives us the confidence that death can be conquered. Hope gives us the assurance that, in Christ, I have conquered it. Faith believes that Jesus rose from the dead; hope believes that, because He did, so will I.

And so it comes down to this: every time some tragic thing happens in this passing, sin-cursed world, am I willing to step back from the pain and trust in the goodness of God even while my heart is breaking? I cannot deny the hurt and remain honest. Nor can I deny God's goodness and remain true. I have to embrace both. "I may die soon, but God is still good." Can I? Will I? That's the question Jesus Himself asked, and continues to ask of us all to this day:

> *"Lord," Martha said to Jesus, "If you had been here, my brother would not have died. But I know that even now God will give you whatever you ask." Jesus said to her, "Your brother will rise again." Martha answered, "I know he will rise again in the resurrection at the last day." Jesus said to her, "I am the resurrection and the life. The one who believes in me will live, even though they die; and whoever lives by believing in me will never die. Do you believe this?" (John 11:21–26)*

I do believe it. And I pray that you will believe it too, right this very second. Because if you do, death, even your own death, will lose its sting in the salve of Christ's salvation. Fearing it no more, you will have a far greater experience in this fair Valley of the Shadow.

Nobody wants to die, but the necessity of it for us all requires at some point that we come to grips with its reality, learn not to fear it, and certainly not to doubt God's goodness because of it. For heaven's sake, behold the great lengths to which He has gone to prove that His love is stronger than death. Through His own great sacrifice He has planted in our hearts the mysterious and wonderful hope of resurrection.

And so my traveling friends, as far as I know my heart in this Valley, I am good with dying. Not because I am brave, but because I know what's on the other side and because my Lord has rebuked inordinate worry. "Do not let your hearts be troubled. You believe in God; believe also in me. My Father's house has many rooms; if that were not so, would I have told you that I am going there to prepare a place for you? And if I go and prepare a place for you, I will come back and take you to be with me that you also may be where I am" (John 14:1–3).

Friends, I sincerely hope and pray that we all live through this cancer. But if we do not, we have nothing to worry about. Death is disarmed by Christian faith. Death is denied by Christian hope. Death is diminished by Christian love.

If this world were all there was and life on this planet was the only life we could live, then for a good God to allow the untimely death of any person would be a great miscarriage of justice. But this world is not all there is. In fact, it's only a brief interlude before the real show, the foyer to our true home which is eternity. As C. S. Lewis puts it in *The Last Battle:*[9] "They were beginning . . . the great story . . . which goes on forever."

We here in the Valley don't think anyone who receives such grace and hope through Christ can stay mad at Him for long. We're standing on the brink of another world, and if Jesus is inviting us over, it would be unmannerly to refuse the promotion.

Your Further up, Further
in Travel Writer,

Pastor Andy

6

HOPE: TOO ACCUSTOMED TO DARKNESS

☼

HOPE SAYS GOD HAS NOT ABANDONED US IN THE WORLD. HIS STORY IS THAT HE PURSUES US, DWELLS IN US, INTERVENES FOR US AND WILL NOT FORGET US WHEN HE FINALLY DETERMINES TO SET THE WORLD TO RIGHTS.[1]

My Dear Fellow Travelers,

Greetings from the Valley of the Shadow! Your intrepid Travel Writer has a report on an interesting point of language use by the locals here and those of you on the outside in the larger world that we've previously nicknamed Myopia. The phrase I have in mind is the well-meaning interrogative often used as a greeting in both cultures: "How are you doing?"

It's such a simple question. And it's kind too, motivated by the desire of the questioner for the well-being of the questioned. Yet those in the Valley tend to hear and answer that question in a different way from those on the outside. I thought I'd use this installment of my Travel Writer missives to give you all a bit of personal insight into how folks on this side think about the "how are you?" query, hereafter designated TQ for The Question.

First, you must realize that to the Valley dweller, TQ is generally a far more complex question than to those who have not yet ventured into the shadow. To them, TQ includes several distinct subsections that may be fuzzily latent in the mind of the asker but which are crystal clear to the mind of those in the Valley. I will break these down by headings and explain them as follows:

1. The basic "I care about you and that's why I'm asking" subsection, here labeled "I CARE." This obviously is more of a statement than a question, and is always much appreciated by the askee. Both cultures, Valley and Myopia, use TQ this way. We're glad to see each other, we care about each other, and that's how we express our fondness. Of course, the proper answer to "I CARE" is "I CARE RIGHT BACK!" So we say, "I'm good buddy, how are *you* doing?!" Slap on the back and goodbye, another friendly interaction!

2. The "are you winning the cancer battle . . . or not?" subsection, here labeled "ARE YOU MAKING IT?" To a person who is in a fight for their life, this is the subsection they sometimes hear when TQ is asked. Right after I'd had a cancerous tumor along with twelve inches of my colon removed and a PET scan showed that the cancer had spread to my lymph system to another tumor near my spine, I encountered two IBC staffers at a meeting who asked me TQ. Concerned that I had cancer cells pulsing unopposed through my veins (I had not yet begun chemo), in my mind I heard them asking the ARE YOU MAKING IT? subquestion and, before I could stop myself, answered it honestly: "At this moment, I have to tell you it doesn't look good . . ." Their shocked expressions immediately let me know that I'd pulled a cultural faux pas. Realizing my error, I laughed and lied, "Just kidding!" Funny thing, word must have got around staff because no one working at IBC has asked me TQ for the last three months. My bad!

3. The "do you feel okay physically or are you about to hurl?" subsection, here labeled "DO YOU FEEL TERRIBLE?" People in the Valley are usually dealing with some sort of pain or discomfort that constantly reminds them of their shadow-dwelling status. So you can understand that sometimes TQ sounds to them like a query

about their physical symptoms. I had a friend who works at a drugstore who made an after-hours delivery to my home of some much needed anti-nausea medicine—a prince of a guy! As he gave me the meds he asked TQ, but in my mind I heard the "DO YOU FEEL TERRIBLE?" subsection and answered honestly: "I'm nauseated, constipated, fatigued, and sleepless most nights . . . yes, I do feel pretty terrible." The look of horror on his face immediately told me I'd made another cultural faux pas. "Well," he stuttered, "thanks for being honest!" "You bet!" I said, secretly kicking myself for yet another TQ mishandling.

4. The "Are you an emotional wreck or are you holding steady?" subsection, here labeled "ARE YOU READY TO GIVE UP?" Many people in the Valley soon realize that their sojourn in the shadow isn't a sprint, but a marathon. They have to come to grips with the reality that they may never again live in Myopia, but that neither might they be passing quickly through the Valley to the golden gates on the other side. Their pain or disability or suffering may go on and on and on for quite a while, and that gets more than tiring. It gets downright discouraging. So when well-meaning friends ask them TQ, they sometimes hear the "ARE YOU READY TO GIVE UP?" subquestion.

   I think this is best answered with actions and not words from Valley dwellers. For me, it comes out in certain (possibly perverse?) ways according to my sense of humor. For instance, I determined from the beginning that the way for me to show I have not given up on the fight is to name the fight and refuse to let it become the elephant in the room. For example, I recently played in a golf tournament with a bunch of my buddies and could tell they were all tiptoeing around my cancer. So I started in on the first hole begging for gimmes with the line, "After all guys, I've got cancer." At first, they caved because that cancer cudgel is formidable. But after the third time I used it on them, they understood what I was doing and retorted, "Forget it dude, make the putt." At that moment I knew that they knew I had not given up because why would I still be trying to take their money on the golf course if I had?

It's like the note I received recently from a friend: "I hope all is well. I wanted to let you know about a really fun opportunity that is coming up. It is called the Undy 5000, and it is a walk/run to raise money for the colon cancer alliance. It is October 31st at Winfrey Point at White Rock Lake in Dallas. I did it last year, and it was really fun. This year, our clinic is doing it in costume. Our team is called: Heinie Herd, so several of us are going as farm animals."

Am I ready to give up? Not as long as the Heinie Herd dressed up like cows and sheep are run-walking to help save my life! Now I'm not only "Semicolon" and "Travel Writer" and "Clipboard King," I am also a "Heinie Herder." Wonderful.

5. The "are you sinking spiritually or is hope still alive" subsection, here labeled "DO YOU STILL HAVE HOPE?" Now we get down to the brass tacks of TQ, both to the askers and the askees. This is, I believe, the most important iteration of the "How are you doing?" question for people here in the Valley. And ironically, this subquestion, while being the most profound of the five, is actually the simplest to answer. One thing Valley dwellers are generally cognizant of is their hope quotient. Hopelessness is a poor agent of self-deception, while hope is a welcome commodity that makes its presence readily felt. So when a Valley dweller with hope is confronted with TQ #5, an accurate and appropriate answer can quite truly be, "I'm fine, thanks."

I had a young friend who asked me TQ after church one day and was clearly disappointed when I gave that simple answer, exhorting me, "C'mon Andy, tell me truthfully, how are you, *really*?!" He was operating under the reasonable assumption that nobody fighting cancer can actually be "fine," and that any indication otherwise was at best naïve optimism and at worst cynically expressed pessimism. He probably expected that an honest answer from me would look more depressingly like this from Barbara Ehrenreich: "But I can report that breast cancer did not make me stronger or more spiritual. What it gave me, if you want to call this a 'gift,' was a very personal, agonizing encounter with an ideological force in American culture that I had not been aware of before—one that encourages us to deny reality, submit cheerfully to misfortune, and blame only ourselves for our fate."[2]

But in point of fact, I actually could answer my young friend's "how are you doing?" inquiry with "I'm fine, thanks" for a very simple but powerful reason. I have hope, and here in the Valley, hope is a very important thing to have. In 1997, Roberto Benigno's Academy Award–winning film *Life Is Beautiful* tells the story of Guido, an Italian Jew who is taken with his five-year-old son Joshua to a Nazi concentration camp. To protect his son from the horror there, Guido creates a game that neutralizes the fearfulness of the camp. The prize for winning, Guido promises, is a real tank! Although Joshua doubts at times, the hope of winning the tank keeps his mind focused on the game rather than on his fear. At the end, the boy, now a man, speaks of his father's greatest gift to him: Hope. What that boy needed, we all need. And like Joshua in the concentration camp, I have One who gave me the priceless gift of hope even in this most unexpected of Valleys.

My friend Scott McClellan writes,

> *Four years ago, this strange micro-trend appeared: A handful of Dallas-area megachurch pastors were diagnosed with cancer within the span of about twelve months. Now, we don't exactly have a shortage of large churches here in Dallas, but still, it was weird and disturbing. It hit closer to home because my pastor was one of the handful. Andy's diagnosis was out of the blue, and it was serious: stage 4 colon cancer by the time they caught it. Grim stuff.*
>
> *From my somewhat removed vantage point, it was odd to see an easygoing, fifty something, Harley-riding pastor suddenly saddled with such a somber malady.*

But Andy, to his credit, remained calm. As one frequently wracked with anxiety, I was curious about the source of Andy's calm. Is he just that confident God will answer all our prayers for healing? I wondered. I figured it had to be that or good old-fashioned denial, but it was neither. A churchwide email from Andy in 2009 explained what was really going on. He wasn't naively optimistic about his health. Stage 4 colon cancer is far too serious to allow that. And as a pastor, he had visited too many hospital rooms and presided over too many funerals to think that any of us get to live forever.

No, Andy wasn't optimistic, but he was hopeful. I realize now that for Christ-followers, the difference between naive optimism and grounded Christian hope is both monumental and monumentally misunderstood. Andy hoped he would beat the cancer and spend a couple more decades here on Earth. He made no bones about that. But the source of his calm was a short phrase in the middle of a passage he quoted from Psalm 39: "My hope is in you."[3]

I have hope, and that hope is in the risen Savior, Jesus Christ. As your Travel Writer, I want you to have hope in Him, too. If He has endured death for us and then came back to life from the grave, then nothing we face as we follow Him can kill hope in our hearts. Such hope is an indispensable commodity here in the Valley. Do you have it? If not, it may mean you need to rethink a hopeless retreat from life just like a couple of Jesus' disciples did right after His crucifixion in Jerusalem. Cleopas and his friend's story of being on the road home to Emmaus with dashed dreams and hopeless hearts is in Luke 24. Their Hope, Jesus, had just died on the cross and been laid in a borrowed tomb. If you had asked them TQ, I'm reasonably sure they'd say, "Terrible!" But it was just then that matters took a surprising turn.

> *Now that same day two of them were going to a village called Emmaus, about seven miles from Jerusalem. They were talking with each other about everything that had happened. As they talked and discussed*

these things with each other, Jesus himself came up and walked along with them; but they were kept from recognizing him. (Luke 24:13–16)

Early that morning on the third day after Jesus' burial, the women had arrived at the tomb to find the body of Jesus missing and two angels asking, "Why do you seek the living One among the dead? He is not here, but He has risen." The women reported these things to the other disciples who disbelieved them. Then these two began the seven-mile walk home to Emmaus. Despairing of hope, they retreated to spiritual darkness. As Frederick Buechner says, "They were so lost in their sad and tangled thoughts that they did not recognize him any more than you and I . . . because, like theirs, our eyes are too accustomed to darkness and our faith not strong enough to believe in the reality of light even if it were to blaze up before us."[4]

Emmaus is as much a state of mind as a place. These two were fleeing the disappointments of Jerusalem. Emmaus was hopeless but predictable; suffocating but safe. Until Jesus intervened, they were going there. Unfortunately, so are many here in the Valley. But in the light of Jesus' resurrection from the dead, none should ever again live in a hopeless, suffocating place.

He asked them, "What are you discussing together as you walk along?" They stood still, their faces downcast. One of them, named Cleopas, asked him, "Are you the only one visiting Jerusalem who does not know the things that have happened there in these days?" "What things?" he asked. "About Jesus of Nazareth," they replied. "He was a prophet, powerful in word and deed before God and all the people. The chief priests and our rulers handed him over to be sentenced to death, and they crucified him; but we had hoped that he was the one who was going to redeem Israel. And what is more, it is the third day since all this took place." (Luke 24:17–21)

The saddest words in our language begin with the letter D: disappointment, doubt, disillusionment, defeat, despair, death. All these concepts show up in the sad words of Cleopas and his companion in that plaintive cry of verse 21: "We had hoped that he was the one who was going to redeem Israel."

Things hadn't gone the way they were supposed to! Life wasn't following the script—the way life is supposed to work as we have all learned from movies. Like how anyone can land a plane because there is always a patient expert in the tower to talk them down, right? A man feels no pain while taking a ferocious beating (but winces when a beautiful woman cleans his wounds!). All bombs have digital readouts so you know exactly when they will explode. *That's* the script!

But in real life, there's not always someone in the control tower, no pain, or readouts on bombs. Real life lacks the poetic justice of the movies, so pain and disappointment skew our perspective. We become accustomed to harshness and believe that is all there is and lose hope. So here are Cleopas and his friend, disappointed and hopeless, eyes blind to the identity of the One walking with them—the risen Lord Jesus! Their physical vision was functional, but they were blinded by their disappointment to truth that would have brought them hope. And so are we.

There's an old story about a man reciting his problems to a friend. He has lost his job, his house, his money, his fiancée—and his friend keeps saying, "It could have been worse, it could have been worse." Finally the man erupts. "How could it be worse?" And his friend mutters, "It could have happened to *me*." Well it *has* happened to us here in the Valley. People lose hope for all kinds of reasons, perhaps a misery-inducing divorce, a hope-shattering rejection, a despair-producing depression, a shame-generating failure, an energy-sapping conflict. Add a cancer diagnosis to that and all bets are off. So TQ, how are you doing? Terrible.

But God has a better ending in mind:

> *In addition, some of our women amazed us. They went to the tomb early this morning but didn't find his body. (Luke 24:22–23)*

So yes, it feels terrible when one day we awake to find ourselves with cancer. But do you see the irony in the conversation on the Emmaus road that day? Cleopas and his friend telling Jesus how bent out of shape they were that Jesus was dead? Yes, the script had changed from their expectations, but in truth the play's climax stayed the same, only *better.* Jesus, the prophet, was alive. Only now, having suffered on the cross and risen from the dead, He had proven not only that He was the Redeemer of Israel but also the Son of God.

I love the way Barbara Taylor connects the dots about this for us. "What I . . . have . . . is a God who resurrects us from the dead, putting an end to it by working through it instead of around it—creating life in the midst of grief, creating love in the midst of loss, creating faith in the midst of despair—resurrecting us from our big and little deaths, showing us by his own example that the only road to Easter morning runs smack through Good Friday."[5]

No, landing here in the Valley may not be what you would have scripted for your life at this point. But as your faithful Travel Writer, I declare that the resurrection of Jesus is God's assurance that His ending is better than any script you or I could ever conceive. We may not like it that Good Friday is part of God's script. But any temptation we may have toward hopeless cynicism is always premature for the simple fact that the cross didn't end in death, but life!

> *They came and told us that they had seen a vision of angels, who said he was alive. Then some of our companions went to the tomb and found it just as the women had said, but they did not see Jesus. (Luke 24:23–24)*

Cleopas and his friend are upset because, despite the reports of an empty tomb, "they did not see Jesus." So we understand that people are error-prone, but now God too? Couldn't the Almighty have raised Jesus as promised? Did the Father just not think this thing through? Could He not have prevented it? And failing that, could He not have fixed it?

This is how dashed dreams lead to hopeless resignation, and hopeless resignation to a fear-filled life.

In *A Tale of Two Cities,* Charles Dickens writes about a doctor imprisoned in the Bastille who kept busy as a cobbler. For twenty years in a dark prison cell, he could be heard at night tap, tap, tapping, repairing the shoes of other prisoners. When the French Revolution came, he was released. But he couldn't cope with freedom. So he prepared a room in his attic that was exactly the same as his prison cell where, every evening, his servant heard him tapping away through the night.

Are you allowing yourself to hole up in a dark attic, bereft of hope, telling yourself you feel secure there? With this cancer, God hasn't fulfilled your expectations, and it just feels too dangerous to you to trust what seems to you to be an unavailable, error-prone God one second longer. As your Travel Writer, I understand because I have been right where you are. The thing to remember right now, though, is that when we feel hopeless and clueless in the Valley, we serve One who has everything under control.

> *He said to them, "How foolish you are, and how slow to believe all that the prophets have spoken! Did not the Messiah have to suffer these things and then enter his glory?" And beginning with Moses and all the Prophets, he explained to them what was said in all the Scriptures concerning himself. (Luke 24:25–27)*

Jesus says the disciples' disillusionment was foolish because they counted as an accident what God had carefully planned from eternity past. God had not failed them, but they thought He had because they had not carefully listened to Him. What seemed a travesty was truly God's gift.

Was the Messiah's suffering an accident? No. See Isaiah 53:10–12. It was all part of God's carefully orchestrated plan to bring glory from pain, encouragement from suffering, and salvation from despair.

Many years ago a philosopher named Pierre Bayle slammed God for the evil that hurts innocent people. He posed a dilemma for people of faith that went like this: If God is good, He would destroy evil. If God is all-powerful, He could destroy evil. But since evil is not destroyed, then God Himself is either evil, or weak, or both.

But when Bayle said that evil is not destroyed, he implied "and it never will be." That is an unwarranted leap. Who sets time limits on God, anyway? Here is what the Word of God teaches: God is all-powerful, and He *can* defeat evil; and because God is good, He *will* defeat evil someday. That is biblical hope—not a shaky wish but a confident expectation that what God has promised will come to pass. Hope is not wishful thinking, but the happy certainty of God's promise.

So when is it appropriate to succumb to despair and retreat to our attic? What is the line that we cross as Christians when it is reasonable to stop hoping for a glorious future by faith? There is none. The line doesn't exist. God's irreversible gift to us in the resurrection and life of His Son Jesus Christ is hope, and hope means never becoming accustomed to darkness. That is what Cleopas and his friend learned and what we all here in the Valley need to learn as well.

> *As they approached the village to which they were going, Jesus continued on as if he were going farther. But they urged him strongly, "Stay with us, for it is nearly evening; the day is almost over." So he went in to stay with them. When he was at the table with them, he took bread, gave thanks, broke it and began to give it to them. Then their eyes were opened and they recognized him, and he disappeared from their sight. They asked each other, "Were not our hearts burning within us while he talked with us on the road and opened the Scriptures to us?" They got up and returned at once to Jerusalem. There they found the Eleven and those with them, assembled together and saying, "It is true! The Lord has risen and has appeared to Simon." Then the two told what had happened on the way, and how Jesus was recognized by them when he broke the bread. (Luke 24:28–35)*

It all comes home to Cleopas and his friend when they sit down to eat with Jesus. As the Lord blesses and breaks the bread, their eyes focus on His hands and they cannot believe what they are seeing there—fresh nail wounds. Suddenly, the truth dawns on them: the amazing teaching they have just received came from the amazing Teacher they had loved and followed and whose death they had grieved. Their strangely veiled companion on the road that glorious day was none other than the risen Lord Himself. And then He was gone.

Cleopas and his friend did not know it, but on the road to Emmaus that day Jesus walked beside them every step. That is why their hearts were burning. God was with them, speaking to them, telling them a better story than the one they were believing. In the same way, He is with you right here, right now, in this Valley, today. And that burning in your heart, that voice telling you that you have grown too accustomed to darkness and that you need to keep hope alive? That is not the voice of a song or a preacher or a Travel Writer. That is *His* voice. The voice of a living Savior. Are you listening to Him? Cleopas and his friend finally did start listening, and the hope that resulted from their hearing Jesus turned them around. "They got up and returned at once to Jerusalem. There they found the Eleven and those with them, assembled together and saying, 'It is true! The Lord has risen . . .' " (Luke 24:33–34).

What was true then is true today right here in this Valley. If Jesus is alive, then hope is real. Jesus' resurrection changes everything! That means that for people of faith, cynicism at life is always premature and disappointment with God is always uninformed. The Savior is alive, and He is walking with you and whispering to you even if you haven't yet recognized Him.

What Valley dwellers want those in the land of Myopia to understand is that yes, it is actually possible for people of faith to stand in shadows and still be fine, just fine, and maybe even better than fine. As a result, answering TQ "Fine, thanks" is not a dismissive or dishonest or superficial

☼

I believe that although the two disciples did not recognize Jesus on the road to Emmaus, Jesus recognized them, that he saw them as if they were the only two people in the world . . . and he also sees each of us like that . . . I believe that whether we recognize him or not, or believe in him or not, or even know his name, again and again he comes and walks a little way with us along whatever road we're following. And I believe that . . . . he offers us a new hope, a new vision of light that not even the dark world can overcome.[6]

answer but a true, genuine, and even miraculous one because it is actually possible to be physically depleted and emotionally exhausted and yet walking steadily forward with faith, hope, and love. One can indeed be living in the Valley and simultaneously "doing just fine."

How can this be so? Randy Alcorn tells the story of the late Pastor James Montgomery Boice who, in May 2000, stood before his Philadelphia church and explained that he'd been diagnosed with liver cancer:

> *"Should you pray for a miracle? Well, you're free to do that, of course. My general impression is that the God who is able to do miracles–and He certainly can–is also able to keep you from getting the problem in the first place. So although miracles do happen, they're rare by definition. Above all, I would say pray for the glory of God. If you think of God glorifying Himself in history and you say, where in all of history has God most glorified Himself? He did it at the cross of Jesus Christ, and it wasn't by delivering Jesus from the cross, though He could have. God is in charge. When things like this come into our lives, they are not accidental. It's not as if God somehow forgot what was going on, and something bad slipped by . . . God is not only the one who is in charge; God is also good. Everything He does is good . . . If God does something in your life, would you change it? If you'd change it, you'd make it worse. It wouldn't be as good."*[7]

I'm reasonably certain that, if you had asked TQ of Dr. Boice right after he said those words, he would have replied, "Fine, thanks," and it would have been a true and honest answer. He was a man of faith, you see, and was resting in God's promises like the following: "God is our refuge and strength, an ever-present help in trouble" (Psalm 46:1). Or how about this one: "Do not fear, for I have redeemed you; I have summoned you by name; you are mine. When you pass through the waters, I will be with you" (Isaiah 43:1b–2a). Or maybe this promise of eternal life in an eternal kingdom to those redeemed by God's grace: "They will be his people, and God himself will be with them and be

As Christians we may or may not receive what we hope for, but the One we hope in stands ready to give of Himself instead. Our health may fail. Our relationships and careers may run off the rails. Armies and economies and nations may collapse under the weight of their power lust. But Christian hope lives because our Redeemer lives.

There will be tears in our eyes, but He will wipe them away. There will be death and decay, but He will cause newness and resurrection to spring forth. While the grave remains—for now—it's hope that erases its victory. And while death remains—for now—it's hope that has wiped out its sting.[8]

their God. He will wipe every tear from their eyes. There will be no more death or mourning or crying or pain" (Revelation 21:3–4).

Would Dr. Boice have preferred not to have cancer? Unless he had become light in his loafers in old age (and I don't think he had), of course he would have preferred health over sickness. But did his sickness mean that he wasn't fine? No. He was just fine, because he had hope. Eight weeks after announcing his illness to the church, and having taught his people first how to live and then how to die, Pastor Boice departed this world to "be with Christ, which is better by far" (Philippians 1:23). He was fine when fighting cancer, and he was fine when he went home. That's a continuous "fine" line. Get it?

Now please understand, neither I nor most of those I know here in the Valley have any plans and certainly no desires for an early exit from life on this planet. What we want you all to know is that if death is the worst case scenario and we can be okay facing that, then surely we can be fine with facing whatever lesser challenges life in the Valley might bring. Got it? And get this too: cancer is not the only difficult condition under which people of faith can be "fine." God's promises and presence and grace are available for us all no matter what hard things are cascading our way. We all have our share of worries and heartaches here in the Valley, but I want you to know that "just fine" living is your birthright through faith in our risen Lord Jesus Christ.

So, to bring our linguistic/cultural discussion to a conclusion, I'd like to review and make a suggestion. We've noted that big problems can ensue when a Valley dweller fails to discern which combination of the five TQ subquestions is actually being asked. For a Valley person to honestly answer a subquestion that was not intended by the asker is to create an awkward moment indeed.

Perhaps a good practical suggestion to Myopians for avoiding these awkward moments is this: please *specify* your subquestion under TQ. Instead of just asking the Valley dweller "How're you doing?," go right for the jugular. Want to know if I feel terrible? Then ask, "Hey Andy, do you just feel terrible?" It's hard to misunderstand such a refreshingly pointed interrogative and I'll have no compunction in giving you an honest answer. You may also want to go with a more positive form of the direct question, "Are you feeling good today?" but don't be shocked if the honest answer comes back the same, "No, actually I feel terrible . . . but you wanted to know, right?" Smile, right here.

Or, if such brutal directness rocks your comfort zone, another suggestion would be to go ahead and ask TQ but resolve in advance not to be aggravated with whatever honest answer your Valley dweller friend might give. We've already talked about the awkwardness of his answering a subquestion that you didn't really want to know the answer to. But you must also resolve not to be offended with what may seem to you a flippant or even superficial answer to TQ, such as, "Fine, thanks," because it can actually be (and probably is) the truest response you could receive. Why? Because . . . "I wait for the Lord, my whole being waits, and in his word I put my hope. I wait for the Lord more than watchmen wait for the morning, more than watchmen wait for the morning" (Psalm 130:5–6).

So why not hear His voice and recognize Him today . . . right here, right now, get off the road to Emmaus and light out for the City of Peace by affirming, "It is true! The Lord has risen . . ."

Your Travel Writer, Doing
Fine, Really,

Pastor Andy

7

TREASURE: THE THINGS THAT MATTER MOST

GOD HAS CREATED YOU IN ORDER THAT YOU MAY GROW TOWARD HIM, THAT YOU MAY REALIZE THE PURPOSE OF YOUR LIFE, THAT YOU MAY RECOGNIZE THE DIVINE IMAGE WHICH CONSTITUTES THE PATTERN OF YOUR EXISTENCE. THE GOAL OF OUR EXISTENCE IS GOD. —THOMAS AQUINAS

Dear Fellow Travelers,

As I mentioned in an earlier note, one of my nurses gave me a bumper sticker (now on my office door) that aptly states: "STUPID CANCER." I love it. I wanted to give you a brief update on how the battle goes, but I warn you in advance that this will again be as exciting as watching paint peel. That's kind of how it goes with these duels with dumb cells. My war began promisingly with all sorts of dash and aplomb—two major surgeries, double-barreled chemo, PET scans, and exotic side effects. There was a lot of news to report in those halcyon days!

But now I have entered the long march phase in which, for the foreseeable future, my updates to you will mainly consist of the following: "Got chemo, had a hard week and then a good week. Got chemo, had a hard week and then a good week. Got chemo, had a hard week and then a good week . . ."

That was the CliffsNotes version of a year's worth of chemo. To be accurate, I should have repeated that phrase many more times. Glad I shortened it for you? That's what I meant about paint peeling. Updates with no real news are more like beat downs. But wait, it's not all bad. The long march has actually served to refocus my mind on a phrase that, though clichéd and overused, is still a profound if simple observation: "Life is a journey not a destination."

In the ordinary course of our days, it doesn't feel that way. Time passes so incrementally that we live as if this world were our destination. Death and eternity seem so distant. Reality is the kids' carpool, the broken garbage disposal, and the latest episode of a favorite TV show. It's only when we see life compressed, life from God's eternal vantage, that it hits us again. Cancer has reminded me to see that way. Time is fleeting. Life is brief, then we go. It truly is a journey, and a rather brief one at that.

Thus our chief concern ought to be making every step of that journey count. Sadly, it's hard to stay aware of ultimate priorities when the urgent, superficial priorities of this life crowd so aggressively into our consciousness. The temporal and the trivial crowd out the eternal and the important.

If we're only passing through this world, then our focus ought to be on the ultimate destination, and that means reviewing from time to time what matters most on the journey. Cancer provides a great opportunity for us to recycle our lives by discovering and pursuing the things that matter most. We're born into this world with a burning question we spend our existence seeking the answer to: what on earth am I here for?

In literature, the quest takes many forms. In the *Gilgamesh* epic, a king

☼

"Throwaway bottles, throwaway cans, throwaway friendships, throwaway fans.

Disposable diapers, disposable plates, disposable people, disposable wastes.

Instant puddings, instant rice, instant intimacy, instant ice.

Plastic dishes, plastic laces, plastic flowers, plastic faces.

Lord of the living, transcending our lives, infuse us with meaning. Recycle our lives."[1]

is questing for eternal life. He fails. Then we have Homer's Odysseus questing for home, Jason and the Argonauts questing for the Golden Fleece, and Parsifal, Sir Galahad, Sir Lancelot, and even Indiana Jones questing for the Holy Grail. They all pretty much flub up. But they shouldn't feel bad. The Star Trek group set out decades ago questing all through the universe, and several spin-offs later, they're still wandering around out there looking for who knows what!

I'm wondering: have *you* found what *you're* looking for? If not, your entrance into the Valley is a great motivation to do so. Confronted now as you are with the brevity of your life, it is a prime time for you to get straight and embrace fully what Valley dwellers have come to see matters most—and that is what you believe, who you are, and what you do in this world.

BELIEVE

What you believe matters most in the Valley because it determines everything about the quality of your journey. By "believe" I don't mean everything you hold true about everything you can think of, but the singular backbone conviction that is the spine of your entire worldview. In *City Slickers*, Jack Palance (Duke Washburn, "Shorty") asked Billy Crystal (Mitch Robbins) if he knew the secret of life. He did not, so Shorty held up one finger. "The secret of life is your finger?" he asked. "No . . . One thing, just one thing," Shorty replied. "But what's the one thing?" "That's what you've got to figure out."[2]

Whether or not you have hope for the future, whatever may come, is determined by that one thing. Whether or not you find meaning in suffering, no matter how difficult, is determined by that one thing. Whether or not you find courage to endure, no matter how arduous the battle, is determined by that one thing. Whether or not your life becomes an inspiration to others, no matter how obscure you may feel, is determined by that one thing.

We Valley dwellers are intensely interested in what the apostle Paul believed the "one thing" is. He states it in Colossians 1:26–27: ". . . the mystery that has been kept hidden for ages and generations, but is now disclosed to the Lord's people. To them God has chosen to make known among the Gentiles the glorious riches of this mystery, which is Christ in you, the hope of glory."

Over the centuries, prophets, sages, philosophers, and revolutionaries have foisted their "one thing" on a gullible world. Life is about wisdom, pleasure, and art, the ancient Greeks said, but greed and rivalry toppled their statues and destroyed their city-states.

Life is about power and conquest, the Romans said. But corruption and indulgence made them vulnerable to the pagan hordes that overran them.

Life is about order and authority, the French said, but vanity and conspicuous consumption birthed the guillotine and the Reign of Terror.

Life is about power and race supremacy, Hitler said, but the Third Reich gave us Auschwitz and Bergen-Belsen.

Life is about equality of ownership, Marx said, but communism birthed the gulag and the Killing Fields.

There's only one prophet, sage, philosopher, and revolutionary whose teachings have stood the test of time, producing civilization, prosperity, and liberty wherever they have gone, and that's Jesus Christ.

Heralded by prophets, celebrated by angels, worshiped by kings, Christ arrived on earth in a humble Bethlehem birth. The King in disguise, He was fully God now become man. We are amazed when we learn who He really is, and when we understand what He really came to do—die in our place so that we can forever live in His. That Jesus is the Son of God who brought us salvation, truth, and purpose in living is that most authentic thing in this world that you can believe. That you do now believe it is among the few things that matter most in this Valley.

In Colossians 1, Paul reveals a further wonderful truth to believe. A "mystery" implies something formerly concealed and now revealed. The glorious truth that God had now made known to Paul is that Christ is available to all people: the Gentiles as well as the Jews. All people can possess "the hope of glory," that coming day when Christ is revealed for who He is and we will share in that glory because we are truly His children. William H. Smith explains why that is important. "One of the most important elements of being a healthy, holy, useful Christian is knowing how much you need the Lord Jesus Christ, how inadequate you are in yourself, and how only by God's grace can you be sufficient for anything. It may take a long time and many hard knocks for more gifted people to realize this reality, but you know it already."[3]

Do you "know it already"? Do you realize how inadequate you are in yourself and how only by God's grace can you be sufficient for anything? Such self-knowledge and humility is often the first gift that living in this Valley affords. If you have never affirmed your belief in Jesus Christ, it is time to fall off the fence. It is time to go with God. It is time to believe in and serve the One who made you, loved you, and redeemed you!

"Christ in you, the hope of glory." Now that is a "one thing" so wonderful and so true and so intuitively right that we can unreservedly devote our lives to living out its implications.

In Jesus Christ, we find the way, the truth, and the life. It's wonderful to know Him, because to know Him is to know the One "in whom are hidden all the treasures of wisdom and knowledge" (Colossians 2:3). And it matters most to know Him, because any quest for fulfillment in this life apart from Jesus is an exercise in futility. As C. S. Lewis put it in *Mere Christianity,* just as an automobile is designed to run on gas, human beings are created to run on God. Neither can work properly apart from the way they were designed. "God cannot give us a happiness and peace apart from himself, because it is not there. There is no such thing."[4]

As your Travel Writer, I hope Jesus is your "one thing" too, or soon will be.

BECOME

Believing in Jesus is the "one thing" that matters most. But it is not the only thing that matters most. Believing is essential. But becoming is critical. To become something better, something worthier, something higher in our lives is part of the quest. In literature, it always has been:

> *The phoenix rises from the ashes. Cinderella rises from the cinders to become a queen. The ugly duckling becomes a beautiful swan. Pinocchio becomes a real boy. The frog becomes a prince. Wretched old Scrooge becomes "as good a friend, as good a master, and as good a man as the good old city knew, or any other good old city, town or borough in the good old world." The Cowardly Lion gets his courage and the Scarecrow gets his brains and the tin Woodman gets a new heart. In hope beyond hope, they are all transformed into the very thing they never thought they could be.*[5]

We need the North Star of the "one thing" in life to guide us home to happiness and heaven. But having found it, we have to align our lives with what we believe. In other words, it matters most that information leads to transformation and that what we believe shapes who we are. D. L. Moody stated, "The Bible was not given to increase our knowledge but to change our lives." The good news is, that is exactly what God wants for each of us. Having believed in Christ, God's plan for us is to be formed in Christ. That is what Paul strived for in his ministry. In Colossians 1:28–29 he writes: "He is the one we proclaim, admonishing and teaching everyone with all wisdom, so that we may present everyone fully mature in Christ. To this end I strenuously contend, with all the energy Christ so powerfully works in me."

It matters most that Christians who have believed in Christ, emulate Christ. But many never do. They mistakenly think that believing is the only thing that matters most. It never occurred to them that becoming validates believing.

It is like a story about the trucker who was hauling five hundred penguins to the zoo. Unfortunately, his truck broke down. He waved down another truck and paid the driver $500 to take the penguins to the zoo. The next day the first truck driver got his truck fixed and drove into town. Just ahead he saw the second truck driver on foot crossing the road with the five hundred penguins waddling single file behind him. He jumped out of his truck, ran up to the guy, and asked, "What's going on? I gave you $500 to take these penguins to the zoo!" The man responded, "I did take them to the zoo. But I had enough money left over so now we're going to the movies."

Oh, they're supposed to be on display at the zoo, not spectators of the zoo! That was a revelation to the truck driver. It would also be a revelation to a lot of Christians. They believe in Christ, but it's never occurred to them that now they're supposed to be transformed to be like Christ! They didn't know they're supposed to be on display as trophies of God's grace, not just spectators warming a church seat. They've forgotten who they are.

Remember who you are, Christian! Remember whose you are, Christians, and who you are becoming! God's goal for us is that we become like Jesus. Our goal is nothing less than spiritual maturity in Christ. And that is going to take all we can give—time, talent, and treasure—for the rest of our lives, however long or short that is.

It proved to be so for Eric Liddell of *Chariots of Fire* fame. His faith was put to the test in the Paris Olympics in the summer of 1924. A member of the British team, Liddell waited excitedly for the posting of the heats for the 100 meters and sprint relays, his best events. He was stunned to learn the preliminary dashes were on Sunday, a day he considered set apart for the Lord. "I'm not running," he flatly declared, and turned his attention instead to the upcoming 200-meter and 400-meter dashes. That Sunday, July 6, Liddell famously preached in a Paris church as the guns sounded for the 100-meter heats. Nevertheless, three days later he finished third in the 200-meter sprint, taking an unexpected bronze medal. Then he quietly made his way through the heats of the 400 meters, though he was not expected to win. Shaking hands with the other finalists, he readied for the race of his life. Arms thrashing, head bobbing and tilted, legs dancing, Liddell ran to victory, five meters ahead of the silver medalist. "The Flying Scotsman" had a gold medal and a world record. But most of all, Eric Liddell had kept his convictions of faith. He'd kept God first, and as a result, he had become a man of character and faith.

Information had led to transformation, just as God had desired. In the Old Testament, God's people built monuments. But in the New Testament, God's people become monuments. "As you come to him, the living Stone . . . you also, like living stones, are being built into a spiritual house to be a holy priesthood . . ." (1 Peter 2:4–5).

Peter says it is not what we believe that ultimately matters, but what we believe that makes us become. It's fine to build monuments to God's greatness in these days. But remember, the greatest monument you can build is not made of brick or stone, but flesh and blood. It is a life fully devoted to the lordship of Jesus Christ. In this Valley, our lives should be a constant witness to the world that the righteous shall live by faith, that God is faithful to the righteous! Your life should be a constant witness to the world that brings others to faith!

SERVE

Paul knew what he believed. Paul knew what he was becoming. And finally, he knew what he was doing. This is the third thing that matters most. "Now I rejoice in what I am suffering for you, and I fill up in my flesh what is still lacking in regard to Christ's afflictions, for the sake of his body, which is the church. I have become its servant by the commission God gave me to present to you the word of God in its fullness" (Colossians 1:24–25).

Paul's believing and becoming worked its way out practically in his life through serving. That's the progression that matters most.

Belief without becoming is mere speculation, and so is becoming without serving. Doing is the natural outcome of true becoming. Doing nothing to serve calls into question whether or not we have truly believed and become. A fruitless life casts suspicion on the life supposedly dedicated to the things that matter most.

One of the most counterintuitive realities of life in the Valley is that God wants this to be the place of your greatest service to His kingdom. All of us are tempted to assume that the malady that brought us to this place also excuses us from serving in this place. It does not. All the Valley does is to put the spotlight on what people of faith do in their lives more than at any other time in their lives. And when they produce fruit, its impact is felt far and wide. That is partly due to lowered expectations. Sympathetic people make no demands from cancer patients. But it is also due to heightened sensibilities. Cancer patients know this time in the Valley is their opportunity to shine. Every effort made, every task accomplished, every ministry of service completed produces fruit a hundredfold.

The next year after winning Olympic glory, Eric Liddell went to China as a teacher and missionary. For the next nineteen years, he ministered faithfully, primarily in obscurity, often traveling on bicycle, braving constant fighting between Chinese warlords and the Japanese in their growing conquest of China. He made many sacrifices to serve God in those days, and "complete surrender" was his way of describing what it took to stay the course.

In March of 1943, Liddell, along with Americans and other Brits, was imprisoned in a Japanese internment camp. He served others in those squalid, hopeless conditions by teaching math and supervising sports programs for the children. He rose early each morning to study his Bible and was the inspiration of everyone in the camp. But his health deteriorated rapidly. A brain tumor ravaged his body with severe headaches. Shortly after his forty-third birthday in January 1945, Liddell collapsed. His last words, spoken to a camp nurse, were

Kent Hughes tells the story of a woman in Africa who became a Christian. Filled with gratitude, she decided to do something for Christ. But she was blind, uneducated, and seventy years old! So she came to her missionary mentor with her French Bible and asked her to underline John 3:16 in red ink. Mystified, the missionary watched as she took that Bible and sat in front of a boys' school. When school dismissed, she would call a boy or two and ask them if they knew French. When they proudly said they did, she said: "Please read the passage underlined in red." When they did, she asked, "Do you know what this means?" And she would explain the gospel to them. That missionary reported that, over the ensuing few years, twenty-four young men met Christ and became pastors due to her work.[6]

"It is complete surrender." Upon learning of Liddell's death, the world noted that all of Scotland mourned. Perhaps they didn't also notice that heaven rejoiced.

Why? Because one who had begun well, finished the same way. Eric Liddell did the things that matter most. He believed and he became and he served. He put God in first place in his heart and kept Him there over all those years. He was never a stranger to God and therefore he became more and more like his Savior. As a result, he never forgot about others and he never got lazy about serving God and others well.

Some might object that if these are truly the things that matter most, Eric Liddell received a paltry payoff in pursuing them. Surely what matters most in life is not what we believe and become and do for God, but rather what we achieve and acquire and gain for ourselves. But it is not.

Believe Him. Be like Him. Serve Him. That is what matters most. Paul knew it. Eric Liddell knew it. Now we do, too.

Long ago, two paddleboats left Memphis at the same time, traveling down the Mississippi River to New Orleans. As they traveled side by side, challenges were made and a race began. Competition became vicious as the two boats roared through the Deep South. One boat began falling behind. Not enough fuel. There had been plenty of coal for the trip, but not enough for a race. As the boat dropped back, an enterprising young sailor took some of the ship's cargo and tossed it into the ovens. When the sailors saw that the supplies burned as well as the coal, they fueled their boat with the material they had been assigned to transport. They won the race but burned their cargo.

In the pilgrimage of life, many unfortunately do the same. They win in the world but along the way lose their faith, destroy their families, and abuse their freedom. Especially here in the Valley, we are tempted to blame our bad decisions on "Stupid Cancer" instead of stupid values. Please don't let that be you! Are you pursuing the things that matter most? Have you settled the "one thing," are you becoming more like

Jesus, and are you serving those around you even through your illness? If not, it's time to recycle. Don't worry, you have all the necessary time to go just as far in this pursuit as God wants you to go. The key is to get started ASAP.

Your Carrying the Cargo
Travel Writer,

Pastor Andy

8

LOVE: THE MOST PRECIOUS THING

☼

YOU MUST BE CONVINCED OF THIS, TRUST IT, AND NEVER FORGET TO REMEMBER. EVERYTHING ELSE WILL PASS AWAY, BUT THE LOVE OF CHRIST IS THE SAME YESTERDAY, TODAY, AND FOREVER. FAITH WILL BECOME VISION, HOPE WILL BECOME POSSESSION, BUT THE LOVE OF JESUS CHRIST THAT IS STRONGER THAN DEATH ENDURES FOREVER. IN THE END, IT IS THE ONE THING YOU CAN HANG ON TO.[1]

My Dear Fellow Travelers,

Life in the Valley has a powerful way of igniting and deepening our love for God and people so we soon see that love itself is the most precious thing here. I believe that it was Paul's own experience in the Valley that prompted his high valuation of love: "If I have a faith that can move mountains, but do not have love, I am nothing" (1 Corinthians 13:2). Paul's perspective on love as "the greatest of these" virtues (v. 13) was forged in the crucible of his pain. His travails in the Valley solidified the value of love in his heart.

As your Travel Writer, I predict the same will happen for you as you journey through the Valley. The physical, spiritual, and emotional strictures we experience in our cancer battle zero our hearts in on love as the most precious thing. If we are willing to acknowledge the depth of God's love to us even here in Cancerland, the inner pressure of our struggles themselves will extrude love outward to others. It is counterintuitive but true: those who acknowledge they are loved though they suffer have the capacity to love at a whole new level.

Jesus demonstrated this for us. He suffered greatly on the cross, and in so doing He loved deeply. In the Valley, we learn to love deeply through suffering as well. Love comes alive in a new and wonderful way in our hearts as the stresses of this journey force us to see love in new light. In this note, I want to equip you with some fundamental insights about love that will serve you well on your journey.

LOVE DIMINISHES DEATH

David Bloom understood this. He was an embedded journalist in Iraq who died suddenly from a pulmonary embolism. David was also a committed Christian. Though he had a strong understanding of the gospel growing up, it was two years before his death when he placed his faith in Jesus Christ as his Savior and Lord. Consequently, on the day he died, David was at peace with himself, his faith, and his family. That peace was reflected in the last message[2] he would ever send to his wife, Melanie, from a desert battlefield. Observe in his note how his own mortality was very much on his mind.

> *Mel, you can't begin to fathom . . . the enormity of the changes I have and am continuing to undergo. God takes you to the depths of your being, until you're at rock bottom, and then, if you turn to Him with utter and blind faith and resolve in your heart and mind to walk only with Him and toward Him, picks you up with your bootstraps and leads you home. I hope and pray that all my guys get out of this in one piece, but I tell you, Mel, I am at peace. Deeply saddened by the*

> *glimpses of death and destruction that I have seen, but at peace with my God and with you . . . Save this note. Look at it a month from now, a year from now, ten years from now. You cannot know now, nor do I, whether you will look back at it with tears, heartbreak, and a sense of anguish and regret over what might have been, or whether you will say he was and is a changed man, God has worked a miracle in our lives. And not to be trite, but that will set me free. God bless you, Melanie. I love you and I know that you love me. Please give the girls a big hug, squeeze them tight, and let them know just how much their daddy loves and cares for them. With love and devotion, Dave*

David understood the power of love well. I know this because he termed it a "miracle" that God had worked in his life. True that. The love that the Lord Jesus displayed for us is indeed miraculous, not only because of what it is, but also because of what it does. It diminishes the power of death. As your Travel Writer, I sorely desire that you will experience this miracle of love as you travel in the Valley.

LOVE CHANGES EVERYTHING

The shadow of death here in this Valley and beyond jars our hearts to recognize the true value of love, the most precious thing of all.

I wish it weren't true, but sometimes it takes dire circumstances to teach our selfish human hearts to love well. It is as if we need to have our hearts pruned by suffering that they may blossom fully in love. Paul indicates the necessity of this progression when he writes, "Not only so, but we also glory in our sufferings, because we know that suffering produces perseverance; perseverance, character; and character, hope. And hope does not disappoint us, because God's love has been poured out into our hearts through the Holy Spirit, who has been given to us" (Romans 5:3–5). God allows His children to endure tribulations to develop spiritual maturity for which love is the ultimate expression. That's right, God wants the result of trusting Him through the hard times to produce in your heart such a wealth of love for Him and for others that you can hardly contain it.

Paul says that God's fourfold formula for producing that love is suffering, perseverance, character, and hope. Suffering (literally, "to be pressed down") wakes us up to eternal values and priorities, perseverance (literally, "to bear up under") tests our resolve to remain in a difficult situation without giving up, and proven character results when the fire of testing burns the dross of worldly values from our souls. People who prove their faithful character before God find God faithful in their distress. He helps them, and their confidence in Him grows into hope—the certainty that God will keep His word. When a person reaches that certainty, love for a faithful God overflows their heart. In short, here's God's formula for love:

ALL YOU CAN TOLERATE +
ONE MORE THING +
GOD'S ENABLEMENT =
LOVE!

Therefore, your status as a Valley dweller not only does not disqualify you from loving well, it amplifies your love and multiplies its impact.

Truly if love changes everything, and it does, then of all people we who travel in the Valley ought to let it. If we can let love change everything, then most certainly we should. And so we come to the next truth about love that your humble Travel Writer wants in your suitcase.

LEARN HOW TO LOVE WELL

A classic line from Charles Schulz's *Peanuts* shows Linus saying, "I love mankind; it's *people* I can't stand!" It may be difficult for us to admit it, but many of us Valley dwellers could have said the exact same thing when we were still living in Myopia. Like many people there, we admired the concept of love more than the practical application

☼

THIS IS WHAT THE LATE JOURNALIST TONY SNOW LEARNED AS HE WAS FIGHTING CANCER IN OUR VALLEY:

Finally, we can let love change everything. When Jesus was faced with the prospect of crucifixion, he grieved not for himself, but for us. He cried for Jerusalem before entering the holy city. From the Cross, he took on the cumulative burden of human sin and weakness, and begged for forgiveness on our behalf.

We get repeated chances to learn that life is not about us—that we acquire purpose and satisfaction by sharing in God's love for others. Sickness gets us partway there. It reminds us of our limitations and dependence. But it also gives us a chance to serve the healthy. A minister friend of mine observes that people suffering grave afflictions often acquire the faith of two people, while loved ones accept the burden of two people's worries and fears.[3]

of love. Applying love in our relationships with God and people was difficult, and even distasteful.

We can all think of examples: the churlish employee we finally encounter after standing in a long line, the neighbors who "share" their music with everyone on the block, the inconsiderate coworker.

By ourselves, we are incapable of attaining love. That is the bad news. The good news is this: God always provides necessary resources for fulfilling the commands He issues. His supernatural power is available to help us love, and it comes to us through His Spirit. "The fruit of the *Spirit* is love" (Galatians 5:22).

We cannot produce the fruit of love by ourselves, but the Spirit of God helps us as we cultivate the conditions in our soul that are conducive to fruit production. It is like the natural process of fruit-bearing. Years ago, we had an apple tree in our backyard that bore hundreds of apples per season. Yet I never heard that tree straining and sweating right before a new apple plopped out on a stem. Fruit was the natural by-product of nutrition from sun, soil, and water (word and prayer), pruning of old dead branches (death to self), and time. The Spirit of God bears the fruit of love in us Valley dwellers by pruning away worldly, temporal distractions through our suffering. And that is where we have a role in making our suffering count. Along with God's Spirit, we prune the branches of our life by saying no to sin and humbling ourselves before others. Over time and under these conditions, God will pour out His love through our hearts. That is when we can say with David Bloom, "God has worked a miracle in our lives."

PAY IT FORWARD TO GOD

The concept embodied in *Pay It Forward* is an especially intriguing one here in the Valley because our travails have sensitized us to the greatness of our privilege to be the recipients of God's love, mercy, and grace. Our appreciation for God's love just makes us keen to pass it on to others. Paul writes, "Let no debt remain outstanding, except the continuing debt to love one another, for whoever loves others has fulfilled the law" (Romans 13:8). God's Word says I am a debtor, and so are you. We owe a debt of love, even though we have cancer. As your Travel Writer, I would say *especially* because we have cancer. I would never have said that before I entered the Valley. But having been here for a while and having sensed the help and hope of Immanuel, I have come to see that love is indeed the most precious thing of all. God distributes love with poignant generosity to us Valley dwellers. We feel it with amazement and long to express it with faithfulness. We deeply desire to pay it forward. And so we should.

God had this idea first and it was born of love. He is the Author of the original act of kindness, which was not random and never stopped giving and has not stopped changing our world since it was accomplished. John describes what God did, and just as importantly, why He did it: "This is how God showed his love among us: He sent his one and only Son into the world that we might live through him. This is love: not that we loved God, but that he loved us and sent his Son as an atoning sacrifice for our sins" (1 John 4:9–10). The Greek word for the love spoken of here is *agape*. Agape is not natural affection, however intense, but a matter of will. God's love is not liking someone as long as they please you. It is loving them even though they hurt, disappoint, or ignore you. That's what Jesus did when He died for our sins on the cross.

Wouldn't you agree that it's unbecoming to be loved lavishly and then parcel out kindness like a miser? To be loved with Snickers bars and to begrudge an M&M to someone in need? To receive the unselfish love of God and then give our love only to those who can benefit us? That tends to be the way it works in Myopia. Love is not a grace we give, but a commodity we invest, as in this love-letter lament: "Dearest Jimmy, No words could ever express the great unhappiness I've felt since breaking our engagement. Please say you'll take me back. No one could ever take your place in my heart, so please forgive me. I love you, I love you, I love you! Yours forever, Marie. P.S. And congratulations on winning the lottery!"

PAY IT FORWARD TO FAMILY

How is the love in your family in these days? May I be so bold as your Travel Writer to say that perhaps God's bringing you to this Valley may be a great gift to your home. Are there bridges that need to be built back to members of your family? God is giving you the gift of this time in the Valley to rebuild them. Are there calls that need to be made, letters written, apologies offered? God is giving you the gift of this time in the Valley to make those calls and write those letters and ask for forgiveness. Don't give up.

Our most precious privilege in the Valley is to love well, especially if that means reconciling with family from whom we have become estranged. The relationships are permanent, but not so the love. That is something that must be worked for, preserved, restored, and cultivated constantly. That is a difficult and even painful prospect, but with God's help we can face it. With God's help we must face it, as C. S. Lewis says: "We shall draw nearer to God, not by trying to avoid the sufferings inherent in all loves, but by accepting them and offering them to Him, throwing away all defensive armour. If our hearts need to be broken, and if He chooses this as the way in which they should break, so be it."[4]

That is what Quincy Jones learned in a visit he made to the Valley. Quincy has had a storied career. He played the French horn at twelve, and by the time he was fifteen was playing professionally with some of the top jazz musicians of his day. He is perhaps best known as the composer of the score for *The Color Purple*. But his success hasn't come easy. He's been married three times, survived two brain surgeries, and endured a complete emotional breakdown. When he needed surgery for an aneurysm, the doctors told him that his chances against recovery were a hundred to one. Miraculously, he survived. Shortly afterward, someone asked him a question for a magazine interview: "What did you start doing differently after your operation?" Quincy's answer: "The first thing I started doing was hugging a lot . . . when you get down to it, the relationships you have with the people you love are the only things that really matter. Everything else is just fluff and frosting and window-dressing."

Quincy Jones is a world-famous multimillionaire. He is powerful in the music industry. He has everything most people think they want. Yet the first thing he did when he survived surgery? Hug a lot. Love well. That is how suffering grounds us in the reality of our weakness in a broken world. But it also introduces us to a deliriously grateful heart for hope that leads to love poured out. How can we not love a God deeply who has so mercifully sustained us through suffering? Our love for Him sloshes out and spills over all those we encounter in the Valley. And so, perhaps counterintuitively, the chief and most precious commodity of those suffering in the Valley is not bitterness, but an epiphany of love that we long to pay forward to God and family.

PAY IT FORWARD TO ALL

While God and family are the primary recipients of our love in the Valley, they are not the only ones. Jesus loved us when we were far from Him, and we pay His love forward to those who also are far from us. How? What is the currency of love? More love. Jesus first loved us, and now it's our responsibility and privilege to pass it on. John tells us how: "This is how we know what love is: Jesus Christ laid down his life for us. And we ought to lay down our lives for our brothers and sisters" (1 John 3:16). Hmmm. Lay down my life? Not too many chances in the routine of life to take a bullet for someone, so what could that mean? Perhaps putting up with someone whose eccentricities are driving me crazy. Laying my life down can include physical sacrifice, but mostly it means putting someone else's needs ahead of my own. This is especially powerful when Valley dwellers do it, because it is so unexpected!

Victor Hugo's *Les Miserables* illustrates the sacrificial love of Jesus and gives us some ideas about how to pay that love forward to everyone around us here in the Valley. It is the story of escaped convict Jean Valjean, imprisoned for twenty years for stealing a loaf of bread. A bishop shows him hospitality, but Valjean repays him by stealing the clergyman's silver. Caught by the constable, he lies. "The silver was a gift." He is returned to the bishop, fully expecting condemnation.

But nothing could prepare him for the shock of hearing the bishop say, "Of course the silver is my gift. But only part. You forgot to take the candlesticks." Amazingly, instead of the prison he deserved, this recipient of grace was given love and freedom and abundance instead. But the bishop tells him one more thing before he leaves. "You must never forget this moment. Your soul, your life, have been bought back. You are not your own. From now on, you belong to God."

And because of grace, Jean Valjean's life does become an act of love. Honoring the promise given to a dying prostitute, he devotes himself to raising her child, Cosette. Loved, he was liberated to love. Graced, he paid it forward.

I can see my way clear to attempting such self-sacrifice on behalf of people I already like. But wait. God's love is unconditional and everyone is invited to the party. So must my love be, and yours—not picky, but inclusive. As the old chorus puts it, all "are precious in His sight." They better be precious in ours, too, or we're not paying forward the true love of God.

When Mother Teresa went out of her convent in Calcutta, she ran into lots of suffering and dying people in the Valley. Her idea for changing her world was to love the "least of these" by holding dying people, giving them grace and dignity in their death. She did not launch healing campaigns, start mass feeding programs, or lobby the Indian government to support the poor. Mother Teresa did what *she* could do as a diminutive Albanian nun living in India. Besides, there were plenty of customers and no competition! Others joined her mission, holding dying people because it was doable and ordinary people could participate. We call her work extraordinary only because she persisted and became famous.

You may think that since you're here in the Valley, you don't have a great way to show love—nothing dramatic, nothing intense, nothing big. After all, you're the one who is sick, so you figure "pay it forward" applies to others but not you. Not so. Your new address here in the Valley gives you a platform to love others that people living routine lives in Myopia can only imagine. Your love becomes more loving *because* you are in the Valley, not *in spite of* the fact that you are sick. What Mother Teresa did, you can do! You know ordinary people in your life even in this Valley—at your doctor's office, espresso bar, chemo lounge, or school who could use a smile, a hello, or a free attention giveaway from an ordinary person just like you—with extraordinary love in your heart. Pay it forward! So are we to do, remember? "We love because he first loved us" (1 John 4:19).

As your Travel Writer, one way that I have found to love people in the Valley is to engage them in a relationship that vibrates with hope and good cheer. Many folks that I know here lead lives devoid of love and laughter because they walk in fear of their cancer diagnosis, often alone. That is why I carry that wonderful pager (that I described to you in chapter 3) everywhere with me. It provides a great icebreaker and conversation-starter with hopeless people that I do not know but wish to love well in the name of Jesus.

That is also why I often wear my hair hat and hillbilly teeth to doctor's appointments and chemo treatments. These are silly accessories with a serious purpose. The hat is actually a joke visor that has a rash of fake hair spilling out the top. When I put it on, people think I'm some sort of aged (the hair is white), unreformed hippie who hasn't seen a barber in ages. And my hillbilly teeth insert makes me look like a chocoholic who never owned a toothbrush or met a dentist. With my whole getup in place, I have found I can truly confound people by affecting a Cambridge British accent that chafes in people's minds with the hat and teeth. It puts them right where I want them: laughing and listening. They want to know why I can have fun with a chemo needle in my arm and why I can have hope even with Stage IV colon cancer.

And I get the chance often to love them well by sharing my hope in Jesus. This is life-giving for me because I have come to see that my greatest privilege in this Valley is to experience and share the love of God. I want you to experience the same blessing, not necessarily by donning a getup but by finding your own opportunities to engage people around you in a relationship of loving encouragement. If you give your life in this way, you will find it anew. As Frederick Buechner observes:

> *Inspection stickers used to have printed on the back, "Drive carefully—the life you save may be your own." That is the wisdom of men in a nutshell. What God says on the other hand is, "The life you save is the life you lose." In other words, the life you clutch, hoard, guard, and play safe with is in the end a life worth little to anybody, including yourself; and only a life given away for love's sake is worth living.*[5]

Yes, we're debtors to God for that most precious thing in this Valley, love. And because He loves us constantly and without end, it is truly our privilege to pay it forward, forever!

Your Travel Writer Paying
it Forward,

Pastor Andy

9

WAIT: STAY IN THE FREEFALL

BE WARY OF INSISTING THAT YOU KNOW BETTER THAN GOD ABOUT WHEN A PRAYER REQUEST SHOULD BE GRANTED. GOD'S DELAYS ARE NOT NECESSARILY DENIALS. HE ALWAYS HAS REASONS FOR HIS NOT YETS.[1]

Dear Fellow Travelers,

With my children, I've found that the most unpopular word in my vocabulary is "NO." But there's a close second. It's "NOT YET!" To my kids, it's only slightly more tragic to hear "You can't have it" than to hear "You have to wait for it." Can I wear makeup? Not yet! Can I shoot a real gun? Not yet! Can I get my tongue pierced? NEVER!

Just because we grow up doesn't mean that waiting gets easier. I suspect most people are frustrated because they have to wait for something big in their lives right now—a mate, a better job, freedom from a bad habit, you name it. This reminds me of something in one of Johnny Hart's *B.C.* cartoons: "Reporter: I see you have one of those fancy new scoreboards . . . Coach: Oh, we've had that all year. Reporter: No kidding? Does it light up and shoot fireworks when you hit a homerun? Coach: I don't know." He's obviously unhappy because he is still waiting to find out.

There's no getting around it, it's just downright hard to wait. And the hardest kind of waiting is waiting for God to answer our prayers. Especially here in the Valley, patience is no piece of cake! My OCD personality would rather have a root canal than wait. Waiting makes my teeth clench, my blood pressure rise, and my face turn red. Of course, we all have to wait: in traffic, at checkout counters, fast-food drive-thrus, the bank, and on hold with an operator in India to straighten out the latest cellphone billing error.

Since arriving in the Valley of the Shadow, I've found the necessity of waiting to be even more pervasive, difficult, and fearful. In my case, going through cancer surgeries and chemotherapy means all sorts of waiting, and often suspense bound up in that waiting. You get a test and have to wait hours for the results. You get a scan and have to agonize for days over the verdict. You start a new chemo protocol and have to wait months for the effects. You have a surgery and have to wait years to see if it saved your life. Is the treatment working? We don't know; we have to wait and see. Is the cancer back? We don't know; we have to wait and see. Am I going to live or die? We don't know; we'll just have to wait and see.

It's hard enough to wait when you're reasonably sure that what you long for is on its way. But it's a good sight harder to cool your jets when you can't be sure that anything good is happening (or ever will).

By all accounts this "waiting-without-knowing" is the biggest smackdown here in the Valley. A pastor friend who just had a tumor removed from the frontal lobe of his brain is waiting on the biopsy results to see if it's malignant. A relative just had a colonoscopy and is waiting to see if the polyps are cancerous. Another friend we've been praying for just wrote this update: "I had my 4-month follow-up MRI this week and found out that the two spots on my brain are continuing to grow. The good news is that they are still growing at a slow pace, and I am still symptom-free. However, once I start experiencing symptoms, I will need surgery again to remove these small tumors. And it's anyone's guess as to when that will be. It could be as long as a few years or as early as tomorrow. Most likely, my doctors will continue the 'wait and see' approach, meaning that I will continue to go in for an MRI every 4 months, unless I present with symptoms before then." What's going to happen to my friends? We don't know, we'll just have to take the wait-and-see approach.

Waiting is also especially hard here in the Valley because the people tend to believe that happiness only comes when we exit the waiting room. We're eager to get what we wait for because we've convinced ourselves that life is no good until we do. And so we wait to live until we're done waiting. Our hope is to quickly get what we wait for so we have to wait no longer. Our assumption is that if we wait long enough, we'll receive all that we wait for and never have to wait again. Thus we naively assume that if we patiently play our cards just right, we'll eventually become problem-free in this problem-plagued world of ours.

But a half-second's thought about that reveals the fallacy. Nobody ever becomes completely problem-free, and therefore much of life will always involve waiting. We wait for the bank to loan us money, to learn the lab results, to start a family, to get our test scores, to receive justice, to see our loved ones have faith in God, to marry, to discern God's will, to have our prayers answered, to be offered a better job, to get well, to win a World Series, to go to heaven.

So if we wait to live until we're done waiting, we'll never really live. All our life we'll wait to live, and when we die, we'll realize we never got around to it!

That's not what God had in mind. He actually has a whole different purpose for our waiting. He actually declares that waiting is one of His choice tools for shaping our character and deepening our faith. No wonder I'm always in a hurry, but God never is! And so, scary as it is, I have found waiting here in the Valley to be illuminating. I used to picture waiting as sitting back bored in a doctor's office reception area, fidgeting and fretting over wasted time and stacked schedules. I used to

☼

A little boy was riding in the car with his dad on a 250-mile trip to go fishing. After the first fifty miles, the excited lad asked if they were almost there. "No," said the dad, "we've got a ways to go yet." Fifty miles later, "Now are we about there?" "No, not yet." About fifty miles later, "We must be there by now, Daddy?" "Sorry son, we have another hundred miles yet." After another fifty miles, "Daddy, am I still going to be four when we get there?"

think of waiting as passive. But no longer. I now see waiting as an active endeavor, a participatory event, a productive task. Therefore as your trusty Travel Writer my advice to you in antsy times is unwaveringly, "Hurry up and wait." You'll find it worth your while and here is why.

THE WAIT: A TIME FOR PREPARATION

Be patient, then, brothers and sisters, until the Lord's coming. See how the farmer waits for the land to yield its valuable crop, patiently waiting for the autumn and spring rains. You too, be patient and stand firm, because the Lord's coming is near. (James 5:7–8)

In this passage, James is writing to persecuted Jewish Christians who were scattered out to the east of Israel. Things weren't going well for them. And God wasn't bailing them out of trouble right away. They felt like many of us do here in the Valley. He was making them wait! His exhortation to the people is "be patient." The verb he uses is a compound word that means literally "have a long temper." We could say it this way: "Put a long fuse on your impatience. Set the timer of your attitude for the long haul!"

Why? Because no difficult situation lasts forever. In fact, the worst case scenario is that your trouble will last only until Christ, who is surely coming, comes. So then, since the Lord is coming, the question is not "How can I get out of this situation right now?" but "How can I use the time I have left wisely?" The answer is, be patient like the farmer while you wait. He understands that the harvest comes only after it has been well-prepared by the autumn and spring rains.

Someone has said that patience is the ability to idle your motor when you feel like stripping your gears. That's right. It is an active, not a passive thing. The motor is still running, but you are not popping the clutch in a fit of frustration. You are not succumbing to a thumb twiddling "Que Sera, Sera" mentality. But neither are you stepping out to act ahead of God's leading and enablement. You are patient because you know that God has a plan for your waiting that is going to produce much good.

The first thing God wants us to do while we wait is prepare. Farmers understand the cycle of the seasons and the way crops grow. While they wait for the time to plant to come, they prepare the field by cultivating, watering, and weeding it. In the same way, God wants us to use our waiting times to prepare our tools and make ready our barns for the coming harvest. So while the crop is coming, we do not resent the time of waiting, but use it productively to get ready.

First Corinthians 3:9 says: "For we are co-workers in God's service; you are God's field, God's building." Interesting! In times of waiting, God views us as the field which He is preparing to produce a good harvest. What is the harvest God wants to produce? The fruit of the Spirit: love and joy and peace and longsuffering and gentleness and goodness and faith and meekness and self-control. God produces these qualities in His children by taking them through the school of waiting.

Noah waited for the rain to come as God had promised it would. Abraham waited decades for God to fulfill His promise of a son. Joseph suffered for fourteen years in prison as an innocent man, waiting for God to elevate him to a position of authority in Egypt. Even Jesus waited for thirty years before He began His ministry. In other words, waiting is another name for an extended education. It was the preparation in each of these lives that God accomplished during those years of waiting that made these men so effective later on.

The Shawshank Redemption is about a man wrongly convicted of murder. He escapes prison by crawling through a sewer line, a journey the narrator describes this way: "He crawled through a river of [dung] and came out clean on the other side."[2] It is counterintuitive but true: sometimes God cleanses us for service by taking us through some very grimy passages. If that's true (and it is!), then our waiting should not be with consternation, but expectation. As did the psalmist, we trust God to prepare us through waiting. "I wait for the Lord, my whole being waits, and in his word I put my hope" (Psalm 130:5).

This being the case, while you wait, learn new skills! Sometimes we assume that God is making us wait because He wants to punish us or because He's forgotten us. We see ourselves as waiting for Him. But could it be that He's waiting for us? Could it be that He has us in a given situation so we can learn a new skill or sharpen our abilities in some way? Absolutely!

My fellow travelers, people can go to prison and come out with a GED, or a law degree. The point is, they use their time of waiting to develop a new skill. You can (and should) do the same thing as, while you wait, you keep busy doing positive things. Be active, not passive! As Paul says in Galatians 6:9, "Let us not become weary in doing good, for at the proper time we will reap a harvest if we do not give up."

Notice the "if"? Don't grow weary and give up! Before you reap you have to sow, so sow the good seeds of preparation by developing your skills and staying active in positive things.

THE WAIT: A TIME FOR MEDITATION

Don't grumble against one another, brothers and sisters, or you will be judged. The Judge is standing at the door! Brothers and sisters, as an example of patience in the face of suffering, take the prophets who spoke in the name of the Lord. (James 5:9–10)

What was it the prophets didn't do? Complain! Some people here in the Valley love to complain. But James tells us that complaining brings God's judgment. Why? It's a backhanded way of insulting God by questioning His goodness, His care, and His wisdom. God's prophets never did that no matter how bad things got. Instead, they listened to what God was saying and spoke honestly to Him from their hearts. From Amos to Malachi, they voiced their concerns to God, asking questions and crying out without pulling punches. But notice their attitude according to James: "suffering and patience." They asked the hard *why* questions, but then, instead of shaking their fists at God, they vested themselves in quiet meditation to seek an answer from Him.

For example, hear Habakkuk as he cries out to God on behalf of his people who had been captured and abused by the ruthless and godless Babylonians: "How long, Lord, must I call for help, but you do not listen? Or cry out to you, 'Violence!' but you do not save?" (Habakkuk 1:2). Habakkuk goes on to ask God the hard *why* questions about his people's having to wait for justice. But then he does what James told us the prophets are famous for: he listened for God to answer! "The Lord is in his holy temple; let all the earth be silent before him" (Habakkuk 2:20).

It is okay to feel bad about your situation and to ask God bluntly about it. But having done so, listen! Let God speak to you as you meditate on Him. That is what Habakkuk did. All of chapter 3 is a meditation upon God's greatness, and in verse 16–18 he says: "I heard and my heart pounded . . . though the fig tree does not bud and there are no grapes on the vines . . . yet I will rejoice in the Lord, I will be joyful in God my Savior."

The principle is this: We won't get an answer from God until we take the time to listen. A relationship with the Father is nurtured in quiet times, not noisy times; in meditation and thoughtfulness, not crisis. "The Lord is good to those who wait for Him, to the person who seeks Him. It is good that he waits silently for the salvation of the Lord . . . let him sit alone and be silent . . ." (Lamentations 3:25–26, 28 NASB). The Valley of the Shadow with all of its inherent waiting is a great place to practice that silence.

Malcolm Muggeridge was a famous journalist and BBC commentator. In the 1930s, he championed the communist cause but later in life found his way to faith in Christ. Shortly before he died, he said to Bill Buckley Jr.: "As an old man, Bill, looking back on one's life, it's one of the things that strikes you most forcibly—that the only thing that's taught one anything is suffering. Not success, not happiness, not anything like that. The only thing that really teaches one what life's about . . . is suffering, affliction."

The last thing you want to do in the Valley is to waste your waiting! So allow your intrepid Travel Writer to suggest that you keep three questions in mind while you wait. Use them as a stimulus to meditation, and you might even write down the answers in a journal to show God you're paying attention.

1. *While I wait, what am I learning about myself?* It's easy to be kind and patient and faithful when things are going our way. But we show our true colors when the chips are down, and frankly, sometimes it takes a painful situation to make us change our ways. Waiting will reveal our heart, and often that's exactly what God wants—not so that we're unhappy, but so we will see areas in which we need to change.

2. *While I wait, what am I learning about others?* Chuck Colson was Richard Nixon's famous hatchet man who became a Christian just before he went to jail for the Watergate cover-up. He founded Prison Fellowship, one of the most dynamic and effective Christian organizations in the world today. That ministry came into being because while Chuck Colson was cooling his heels in the slammer, he learned a great deal about the men with whom he was incarcerated. He learned that they were real human beings—troubled criminals, but with feelings and hopes and needs. He learned that they too needed Christ. He learned that their lives, like his, could be transformed by the power of God's love. Because he listened and learned about others while he waited, Chuck Colson gained the wisdom and insight to begin his life's work of prison ministry, a calling he would have missed entirely had it not been for his own incarceration.

3. *While I wait, what am I learning about God?* It's often in the calm back roads of waiting that God teaches us the things about Himself that we'll need later to serve Him well. Specifically, we need to learn to depend on Him. Dr. J. I. Packer expresses this well.

> *When we walk along a clear road feeling fine, and someone takes our arm to help us, likely we would impatiently shake him off; but when we are caught in rough country in the dark, with a storm brewing and our strength spent, and someone takes our arm to help us, we would thankfully lean on him. And God wants us to feel that our way through life is rough and perplexing, so that we may learn to lean on him thankfully. Therefore he takes steps to drive us out of self-confidence to trust in himself, to—in the classic scriptural phrase for the secret of the godly man's life—"wait on the Lord."*[3]

This proved out in the life of the young shepherd David, caring for his father's flocks on the hills around Bethlehem. In defending the sheep, he learned that God was faithful: God gave him strength and skill to slay a lion and a bear. So later, when David stood up to the giant Goliath who had intimidated the armies of Israel, he explained his courage by saying, "The Lord who rescued me from the paw of the lion and the paw of the bear will rescue me from the hand of this Philistine" (1 Samuel 17:37).

THE WAIT: A TIME FOR COOPERATION

> *As you know, we count as blessed those who have persevered. You have heard of Job's perseverance and have seen what the Lord finally brought about. The Lord is full of compassion and mercy. (James 5:11)*

The last example James gives us of how to handle waiting is that of Job, who at one point was one of the world's most wealthy and devout men. The book of Job recounts how God allowed Satan to strip Job of his wealth, his children, and his health. So bad was the situation that his heartbroken wife understandably advised him to curse God and die. But Job's response is found in 1:21–22: " 'The Lord gave and the Lord has taken away; may the name of the Lord be praised.' Through all this Job did not sin nor did he blame God."

In fact, later he uttered those often quoted words: "Though he slay me, yet will I hope in him" (13:15). Job had every reason to resist God, but he chose to cooperate. When James reminds us of Job's perseverance, he's using a compound word in Greek literally meaning "to wait underneath." Think of lugging or holding something heavy while you're waiting for instructions on where to place it. That is biblical perseverance, and that is what God wants of us all when we wait!

I think our tendency when we have to wait for God's answers in our life is to kick back and become rebellious. First we worry: "This sure is taking God a long time!" Then we wonder: "Do you suppose God really knows what He is doing?" Then we whine: "God is not answering my prayers or solving my problems. I guess He just doesn't care about me anymore!" We get stubborn and dig in our heels and say, "God, I'm not moving until You do something about this." The end result is that we refuse to cooperate with the only One who can really help us!

So you are childless and God has told you to wait for a baby. You are single and God has told you to wait for a mate. You are ill and God has told you to wait for healing. You are troubled and God has told you to wait for peace. That is tough, but remember that at least as important as the things we wait for is the work God does in us while we wait.

Here is the greatest mystery of waiting: it is really God who is doing it! He is waiting for us to learn, to grow, to trust, to change, and become the people He wants us to be. Our Lord's most famous picture of God's love is of a father in front of his house, eyes fixed on the horizon, waiting for his foolish son to come home (Luke 15). Each of us, in his or her own way, is that son or daughter. We sojourn in the far country, peeved that God is making us wait, when all the time it is He that is waiting for us. The pain of waiting is actually a good occasion for us to come home to all the Father wants to do in our lives. For if we do, we're promised even greater things to wait for in time to come. "I consider that our present sufferings are not worth comparing with the glory that will be revealed in us" (Romans 8:18), Paul says.

Note the words "sufferings" and "glory." Paul invites us to make a comparison of the two. His point? If you could put all the difficulties and pain and suffering of your life on one side of a scale, and the glory that will someday be revealed to you on the other side, the glory would be so much heavier than your present sufferings that they would be blown away like a feather. The sufferings of this life, though terrible, are virtually nothing in comparison with the great weight of glory coming to the waiting children of God. In other words, the anxious longing and eager waiting in spite of pain and suffering is not an unfair burden. Heaven is worth the wait! As someone has said, "Sorrow looks back. Worry looks around. Faith looks up."

Seeking God while we wait involves making faith choices. Sure, there is not yet peace everywhere and all pain has not yet been taken away. But still, we hear voices that pray, notice moments of forgiveness, and witness many signs of hope. We don't have to wait until all is well, but can celebrate every little hint of the kingdom that is at hand. This again is a real discipline. It requires choosing for the light even when there is much darkness to frighten us, choosing for life even when the forces of death are so visible, and choosing for the truth even when we are surrounded with lies. Wise are those who so choose.

The key truth to remember is that God's delays are not God's denials. The genius of Job is that, though he had a tough situation with no solutions in sight, he did not give up on God or rebel against Him. He knew there was a huge difference between "no" and "not yet," and he cooperated with God to make the "not yet" "now"! In short, Job cooperated with God because he chose to maintain HOPE (holding on, praying expectantly).

Here's the central challenge for all who wait in the Valley: can you trust God while you wait by cooperating, not conflicting? Please hear and accept what God is saying to you through this time of waiting in your life. He has reasons for His "not yets." If the request you're making of God is wrong, God says "no"; if the timing is wrong, God says "slow"; if you have the wrong attitude or motive, God says "grow"; but if the request and timing and attitude are all right, God says "GO!"

Never bail out until God has had a chance to finish what He is doing. Some of history's greatest faux pas have occurred because people got impatient and took matters into their own hands. We've got to trust Him, not only with the what, but with the when as well.

Rebekah Lyons writes about what it must have been like for Jesus in the garden of Gethsemane on the eve of the crucifixion.

> *Jesus knew rescue wouldn't come in the way he might have wanted it. It would not come that night in the garden. That wouldn't be the story of rescue to be told through the ages. No, this story required him to stay and yield to the pain.*
>
> *Sooner or later, we all experience a moment in our lives when everything changes. When we realize life doesn't look the way we expected it to. Or what we dreamed it would be. Suddenly we are faced with a moment of crisis. When our painful season becomes indefinite, we lament, questioning how long we must wait for rescue to come. Everything in us wants to run, to escape the pain we are experiencing, to look for ways to numb when it becomes too much to bear.*
>
> *Stay in the freefall. You think you know, but you have no idea.*
>
> *Isn't that what faith is all about? To surrender our will to the One who sees it all? Because we trust he is working something out so beau-*

tiful and beyond our wildest imagination. Jesus, in the flesh, joined our sufferings in life and death. But on that third morning at dawn, he gave us an example of what that exceeding abundance looks like. A promise of hope for all who believe.[4]

Taking a proactive view of waiting is (admittedly) scary and hard. But it still beats the alternative, which is a passive view of waiting that feels safer and easier but leads nowhere good.

The purpose of a waiting room is not waiting. The waiting room is really the living room, and if you put off living until the waiting is done, you will never live. Sure, you'll take up space and show vital signs. But you'll miss the joy, the fruitfulness, and the meaning of life. So please don't shut down when waiting in this Valley, passively longing for the waiting to be done. Persevere with the conviction that God is doing significant work in and through your life in times of waiting. Learn to say with the prophet: "I wait confidently for God" (Micah 7:7 NLT).

I frankly don't know why God has not yet answered some of the most fervent prayers I have offered in this cancer battle. But He is in control, and I'm going to trust Him. "He who began a good work in you will carry it on to completion until the day of Christ Jesus" (Philippians 1:6). That is enough for me! God is working, and I can be confident that He won't quit until the job is done. Someday, it will be! Just not yet. "These things I plan won't happen right away. Slowly, steadily, surely, the time approaches when the vision will be fulfilled. If it seems slow, do not despair, for these things will surely come to pass. Just be patient! They will not be overdue a single day!" (Habakkuk 2:3 TLB).

What are you waiting on God for today? I know you are in a tough situation with seemingly no end in sight. Just remember, God has you here for a purpose and perhaps it is not you waiting for Him, it is Him waiting for you. So give attention to the preparation, meditation, and cooperation of waiting until God has accomplished all of His purposes in you for this time. The bottom line is that those who are patient in waiting times benefit greatly by discovering that God is never overdue a single day (and that they will still be four when they get where God wants them to be).

Your "Embracing the Wait"
Travel Writer,

Pastor Andy

10

LIVE: ALL THE TIME THERE IS

TO REGAIN FOOTING, REMEMBER THAT WE WERE BORN NOT INTO DEATH, BUT INTO LIFE—AND THAT THE JOURNEY CONTINUES AFTER WE HAVE FINISHED OUR DAYS ON THIS EARTH. THOSE WHO HAVE BEEN STRICKEN ENJOY THE SPECIAL PRIVILEGE OF BEING ABLE TO FIGHT WITH THEIR MIGHT, MAIN, AND FAITH TO LIVE—FULLY, RICHLY, EXUBERANTLY—NO MATTER HOW THEIR DAYS MAY BE NUMBERED."[1]

My Dear Fellow Travelers,

Not only have I discovered that people in the Valley grow more introspective the longer they are here, they grow more retrospective as well. That includes me. Evidently our new familiarity with mortality in this place inspires reflection on history. When we come to grips with the possibility that our journey may soon end, we feel compelled to reflect on how well we have made the trip. So I was reminiscing with another friend in the Valley about our individual experiences as dads in raising our children. In my mind's eye, I could see each of my five kids at about age three. I waxed a bit misty recalling the touch of their little hands as they slipped into mine for a walk into Kroger's or the mini-weight of their slight frames plopping into my lap for a fourteenth viewing of *VeggieTales.*

I found myself longing to go back to that place and feel the joy of my little ones as little ones all over again. The funny thing is that when I was actually there with my tykes in the toddler years, I don't remember feeling joy so much as a nagging impatience to be with them sometime beyond that stage. I do remember my heroic wife, Alice, as we subconsciously wondered if, by having five children age twelve and under, we had bitten off more than we could chew. I remember thinking, "If only these kids were more grown up, life would be way better."

If only.

If only we didn't spend more on Gerbers than burgers. If only we didn't have the semipermanent faint odor of hand wipes and the discomfort of hauling soiled diapers to the curb in fifty-gallon bags. If only getting five kids into seat belts and a booster seat and our ancient kids' car seat (with its eight loops, four buckles, and an overhead boom that got stuck on cheddar cheese goldfish cracker crumbs perennially wedged in the hinge) didn't take fifteen minutes every time we went out of the driveway. If only there were no such thing as night fevers and tubes in ears and colic and skinned knees and bumped heads and scraped elbows and fat lips and owies of every size, location, and description. If only there were no terrible twos, and babies could tell you what hurts, and children's clothes didn't sell for Neiman Marcus prices. If only we did not leave restaurants embarrassed by the hundred-square-foot area of food detritus around our baby's high chair. If only, life would be better. If only "if only" would ever come!

NEVERTHELESS

Yet here I was years later, ruminating not on leaky diapers and expensive kids' co-pays and how a pair of high-priced children's shoes didn't last six months, but on those moments of joy in between the not-so-fun stuff that made our family's life full and happy and even holy. And it dawned on me. Fullness of life doesn't come in the "if only," but in the "nevertheless."

The land of "if only" is a shimmering miasma, a fantastic mirage, a cruel hallucination. This is not because no "if onlys" ever come true, but because when they do, new ones inevitably spring up in their place. The default mode of the human soul is to never be completely satisfied, to never be quite content, to always be yearning for that just a little bit more "if only" that we're sure will push us over the top to the perfect life.

We may not voice it consciously, but in our hearts we have driven down a stake of stubbornness. "I won't act, I won't trust, I won't have joy, I won't step out in faith, I won't be happy, I won't love and serve others, I won't be content. How can I? Until You, God, fix what's wrong in my life, how can You expect me to live that life for You? And so Lord, count me in if only You give me a spouse, because I'm lonely. Count me in if only I get that raise, because I'm broke. Count me in if only I manage to graduate, because I'm ambitious. Count me in if only I get the appointment, because I'm deserving. Count me in if only I receive the award, because I'm underappreciated. Count me in if only You heal me of cancer, because I'm sick of being sick. Fix me Lord, then I'll serve; complete the if-onlys, then I'll truly start to live."

But consider how Jesus responded to those who made excuses to delay fully following Him:

> *On the road someone asked if he could go along. "I'll go with you, wherever," he said. Jesus was curt: "Are you ready to rough it? We're not staying in the best inns, you know." Jesus said to another, "Follow me." He said, "Certainly, but first excuse me for a couple of days, please. I have to make arrangements for my father's funeral." Jesus refused. "First things first. Your business is life, not death. And life is urgent: Announce God's kingdom!" Then another said, "I'm ready to follow you, Master, but first excuse me while I get things straightened out at home."*

Jesus said, "No procrastination. No backward looks. You can't put God's kingdom off till tomorrow. Seize the day." (Luke 9:57–62 MSG)

"Follow You Jesus? Love to! And I would, you know, if only the accommodations were five-star, and if only all my family issues were resolved, and if only all the paperwork was finished. After *that,* this; after *them,* You. I promise. (And if You could just grease the skids to make this happen sooner rather than later, then that is all the faster I am in the game for You . . . how about it, Lord?)"

I cringe to think how many times in my life I have intimated those words to God. What I see in them is a whiny, weak, self-regarding follower of Christ who has become too lazy to take up my cross and follow Him. Now that I find myself in the Valley, the temptation to such passivity is even worse. In the past I have had all sorts of good excuses for succumbing to hopeless laziness and abandoning the quest to live a full life of love and faith and service to my King. But now in the Valley, I have the best of all excuses: Stage IV colon cancer. Case closed.

Surely God does not expect me to keep pressing ahead to live life as fully as I can when I am not feeling my best. Surely being in the Valley means Strato-loungers and Netflix, not prayer and loving service. But I cannot escape Jesus' words which grant no quarter from life to people who suffer, even those of us here in the Valley: "Are you ready to rough it? . . . Follow Me . . . First things first. Your business is life, not death. And life is urgent: Announce God's kingdom!"

"Andy, even though you are in the Valley," I hear Him saying to me, "your business is life not death. Even though cancer is tragic, your life is still urgent. Even though you feel like lying down and giving up, I say rough it and follow Me."

JESUS' UNIQUE CALL

It will mean the toughest thing you and I have ever done, too. "You mean I can't procrastinate seeking to live a kingdom life until I'm married or my kids are out of diapers or I'm finally through school? I'd be a much more kind, patient, and cheerful disciple." "Anything but wait!" "You mean I can't delay a contented life until I've finished my master's and have that career and high-paying job with some actual money coming in? I could find satisfaction quicker in a nice new condo than my old apartment with the black mold at the cornices." "Anything but wait!" "You mean I can't wait to start loving and living and serving and trusting and working until the cancer is gone and I feel better? I could do a way better job feeling healthy than sick, you know." "Anything but wait!" Now is the time. Today is the day to live. For today is where our great God of comfort and grace resides.

This is the part of carpe diem that Robin Williams missed in *The Dead Poets' Society*. It is a fine thing to seize the day. Jesus heartily advocates it! What makes Jesus' call unique is that carpe diem comes in the context of unresolved issues, uncompleted dreams, unmitigated tensions, and unfulfilled goals. Seize the day anyway, Jesus says. Follow Me "nevertheless," not "if only." First things first! "You can't put God's kingdom off till tomorrow." Even if I have cancer? Yes, even if you have cancer.

What Christ wants to hear from you is what He has heard from His faithful ones over the centuries as expressed by Paul:

> *We always carry around in our body the death of Jesus, so that the life of Jesus may also be revealed in our body. For we who are alive are always being given over to death for Jesus' sake, so that his life may also be revealed in our mortal body. So then, death is at work in us, but life is at work in you. (2 Corinthians 4:10–12)*

This seems like such a contradiction, and to the unbelieving world it makes no sense at all. The Christian lives and dies at the same time? Yes. While we are dying, we are living. Only it is the life of Jesus living in us. This is precisely the sort of supernatural reality that Myopic outsiders simply cannot understand. Ironically, the more Paul dies in the Valley, the more he lives because Christ lives in him. What exactly does

☼

It was spring, but it was summer I wanted—the warm days and the great outdoors. It was summer, but it was fall I wanted—the colorful leaves and the cool, dry air. It was fall, but it was winter I wanted—the beautiful snow and the joy of the holiday season. It was winter, but it was spring I wanted—the warmth and the blossoming of nature. I was a child, but it was adulthood I wanted—the freedom and the respect. I was twenty, but it was thirty I wanted—to be mature and sophisticated. I was middle-aged, but it was twenty I wanted—the youth and the free spirit. I was retired, but it was middle-age I wanted—the presence of mind without limitations. My life was over—but I never got what I wanted.[2]

he mean by this? I think the answer comes in the twice repeated word "body." It is the body that slowly dies, and it is in the dying body that the life of Christ is clearly seen. When Clarence Jordan wrote his Cotton Patch[3] version of 2 Corinthians 4, he gave us this wonderful paraphrase of verse 11: "We who live for Jesus always flirt with death, in order that Jesus' life may be all the more evident in our fragile flesh."

That is simply fabulous, is it not? We "flirt with death" so that Jesus' life can be seen in our "fragile flesh."

Paul gives us a list of these flirtations with death he had endured in his Valley and that made Christ's life in him even more evident.

> *Five times I received from the Jews the forty lashes minus one. Three times I was beaten with rods,*
> *Once I was pelted with stones,*
> *Three times I was shipwrecked,*
> *I spent a night and a day in the open sea,*
> *I have been constantly on the move.*
> *I have been in danger from rivers,*
> *In danger from bandits,*
> *In danger from my fellow Jews,*
> *In danger from Gentiles;*
> *In danger in the city,*
> *In danger in the country,*
> *In danger at sea;*
> *And in danger from false believers.*
> *I have labored and toiled and have often gone without sleep;*
> *I have known hunger and thirst and have often gone without food;*
> *I have been cold and naked.* (2 Corinthians 11:24–27)

What kept Paul going under the tremendous pressures he bore? Why did he not just give up, call it a day, and find a hammock? Remember his simple and profound reason: "We always carry around in our body the death of Jesus, so that the life of Jesus may also be revealed in our body."

Paul is not bragging on himself. He just wants everyone to know that what happened to him had happened for a reason so that through those hardships the life of Jesus might be clearly seen in him.

So it is with us in the Valley. Our trials serve to provide a backdrop for the living power of Christ. But only if we live "nevertheless" and not "if only" lives. Our cancer battle is not an excuse for exiting the fight to live fully but an opportunity to live nobly and well for as long as we do live. It actually becomes our red badge of courage in pursuing that battle more vigorously than ever before.

HOW TO LIVE WITH ALL YOUR MIGHT

When the great Puritan scholar and pastor Jonathan Edwards was a freshman at Harvard, he wrote seventy resolutions to guide his life. Number six was, "Resolved, to live with all my might, while I do live." I love that. It's succinct, realistic, and visionary. It's "anything but wait." It's "nevertheless" and not "if only." It is realistic in that Edwards assumes the inevitability of death. In the same way, in some of Paul's last words he defined his desire to live with all his might while he did live. The beautiful thing about Paul is that he not only gave us the what, but the how.

> *I have fought the good fight, I have finished the race, I have kept the faith. Now there is in store for me the crown of righteousness, which the Lord, the righteous Judge, will award to me on that day—and not only to me, but also to all who have longed for his appearing. (2 Timothy 4:7–8)*

Was Paul afraid to die? No. One reason that Paul did not fear death was that he had truly lived. Here is his own life summary that describes how he fought to live with all his might even in the Valley, and how you and I can do the same.

FIGHT THE GOOD FIGHT

Paul's life as a Christian was a continual struggle. Note how he described his life: "Rather, as servants of God we commend ourselves in every way: in great endurance; in troubles, hardships and distresses; in beatings, imprisonments and riots; in hard work, sleepless nights and hunger" (2 Corinthians 6:4–5). In other passages he spoke of the spiritual opposition he faced—Satan, the forces of darkness, the indwelling power of the flesh, and the spiritual darkness of paganism.

But in spite of the incredible conflicts in his life, Paul never stopped fighting for Jesus until the day he died. Now at last the struggle is almost over. Soon his Commander in Chief would grant an honorable discharge from the battles of life. Paul had fought well and for him, the battle would soon be over.

Paul understood that life in this world for a committed believer is never going to be calm sailing through peaceful seas. We are in a spiritual battle with the forces of evil that oppose our God and all who serve Him. So Paul understood that hardship and suffering are perfectly consistent with a believer's obedience. The issue for him was not inevitable hardship for Christians, but our reaction to inevitable hardship.

> *Whatever happens, conduct yourselves in a manner worthy of the gospel of Christ . . . For it has been granted to you on behalf of Christ not only to believe in him, but also to suffer for him. (Philippians 1:27, 29)*

FINISH YOUR RACE

"I have fought the good fight, I have finished the race . . ." (2 Timothy 4:7).

Paul was focused on finishing well. To him, the main ingredient of finishing well was, simply, finishing. He knew what we all know, that it is far easier to begin than to end, to start than to finish. It is far more fun to initiate a new project in excitement and optimism than to put nose to grindstone when the going gets tough and complete what you began. That goes for life itself. Living fully in faith right through the final tape of the race of life is one of the most unheralded of all great achievements. One may have blazing speed in the Olympic hundred-meter dash, but no medals are awarded for being first at the ninety-five-meter mark. You have to run all the way, break the tape, and finish the course. Then and only then comes the gold.

In Acts 20:24 (NASB), Paul uses another phrase for "finishing" as he speaks to the leaders of the Ephesian church: "I do not consider my life of any account as dear to myself, so that I may finish my course and the ministry which I received from the Lord Jesus, to testify solemnly of the gospel of the grace of God."

Not only did Paul want to finish the full race. He also wanted to finish the right race. He wanted a completed life that had also been a directed life. "I have finished my course." This is not like Frank Sinatra singing, "I did it my way." Paul means that he followed the course the Lord Jesus set out for him the day He saved him on the road to Damascus. Whether in good times or bad times, Paul had walked in the way of the Lord, seeking to "finish my course." Now that journey was almost over. He could look back and say, "It wasn't easy, it was often hard, and sometimes I wondered if I would make it, but now I can see that Jesus led me all the way." He had finished his course. That is living with all your might! That is not just starting enthusiastically, but finishing directionally and definitively. That is what we must emulate as we move through the Valley.

A professor at a Christian college along with his son went on a thousand-mile backpacking trip from British Columbia to southern California. Together father and son hiked through the mountains of Washington, Oregon, and California. For many days they were alone on the trail, often camping above the ten-thousand-foot level. They faced every sort of discouragement: lack of food and water, danger from wild animals, danger from crazy people they might meet, days of rain and mud, incredible physical exhaustion, the very real possibility

☼

AS A BRIGHT, ATHLETIC HIGH SCHOOL STUDENT JONI EARECKSON TADA WAS PARALYZED FROM THE NECK DOWN IN A DIVING ACCIDENT. THROUGH YEARS OF SUFFERING, HOWEVER, JONI HAS LEARNED CONTENTMENT BY DRAWING ON CHRIST'S STRENGTH.

There are some days when I feel like resigning from being paralyzed. Some days my weak shoulder muscles ache from holding up my heavy (notice I didn't say "big") head. When my back gets tired from sitting and my neck gets a crick from looking up at everybody who stands, I wonder how I've managed to live these past years in contentment. The very idea of spending [many more] years in a chair gives me the shivers. But I have learned the secret of being content . . . God's grace is more than sufficient. And what's more, He doesn't expect me to accept what will happen . . . years from now. I'm content—even joyful—now, knowing that God only gives me grace for today. Right now. This moment. Tomorrow will take care of itself.[4]

of physical injury, not to speak of loneliness, blisters, mosquitoes, and the extremes of heat and cold. Yet this father and son made it. Against all odds, they finished their thousand-mile trek.

Here is the secret of their success. Before leaving on the trip, the professor discovered that over 90 percent of those who set out to hike more than five hundred miles never make it. Fifty percent never get started, and 40 percent quit after they start. Only 10 percent ever finish a long-distance hike. After studying the 10 percent who succeed, he discovered that they made two important decisions: First, they decided they would finish the trip no matter what happened, and second, they expected bad things to happen and decided they would not be surprised or dismayed. The father and son solemnly made those two pivotal decisions before they set out.

So when the rains turned the trail into a quagmire, the father and son did not quit because they were not surprised. When black clouds of mosquitoes descended like an Old Testament plague, they did not quit because they were not surprised. When they faced days of loneliness and nights of hunger, they did not quit because they knew it would be like this. In essence, the successful backpackers adopted a certain mindset. They knew that the key was simply putting one foot in front of the other. You take a step and hit the mud. You take another step and see a bear. You take another step and your legs begin to cramp. You take another step and the crazy people come out of the woods. It does not matter. You are not surprised, because you knew the crazy people would show up sooner or later. So you just keep putting one foot in front of the other and eventually your journey is finished.

This was Paul's approach to the Christian life. No matter what happened to him, he just kept moving forward by the grace of God. One foot in front of the other, one step at a time, one day at a time. He wasn't deterred by opposition because he was determined to finish the race set before him. So was Joseph in an Egyptian dungeon. And David in the cave of Adullam, cold, scared, and hungry from fleeing a man he would have given his life for! And Daniel surrounded by prowling lions dreaming of Daniel dumplings. And three Hebrew youths in a fiery furnace—alive and not alone. Two constants seemed to follow these faithful heroes: hardship and hope. It was always their hope that overcame their hardships. So shall it be for us in the Valley as well.

KEEP THE FAITH

"I have fought the good fight, I have finished the race, I have kept the faith."

Paul "kept the faith." This simply means he refused to compromise the truth in his heart because of the pain in his body. When other people fell away, Paul preached the Word. When the world was against him, Paul paid no attention. When it would have been easy to trim his message to save his own life, Paul proclaimed the whole counsel of God. He did not back down, he did not compromise, he did not retreat or defect, and he did not capitulate to bitter resignation. He kept the faith.

As we have seen, Paul wasn't strong enough in himself to do these things, and neither will we be. He was strong through Jesus Christ. He had learned the lesson of drawing on Christ's power through faith. Through faith, we can endure with hope, even in this Valley. Because Paul knew that nothing could touch him that did not come from the hand of God, he never gave in to discouragement. He truly believed that everything that happened to him was for his good and for God's glory. Therefore, he kept on going for God to the very end. He stayed faithful to the very end. He lived with all of his might, while he did live.

Jane Florence was my friend. Never a more vibrant, positive, loving, life-affirming person could you ever hope to know. She loved Christ and she loved Dan, husband of almost fifty years, and she loved her son and daughter more than life itself. Just six months ago, Jane came to the Valley. My, how valiantly she fought the good fight. How definitively she finished her race. And how magnificently she kept the faith!

One of the most unusual but wonderful things that I've often had the privilege of doing as a pastor is talking to the dying about their impending death. I say it is a wonderful thing. Actually, it is more than that for me. It is a sacred thing. To look into the eyes of a brother or sister who will soon be in heaven and ask them if they are afraid, or are they ready, or who they will look for first when they have crossed over, or what they want me to say on their behalf at their funeral. With believers in Christ, I have the most incredible conversations because they are indeed ready and they are most certainly unafraid and they are most magnificently inspiring. Jane made me weep with joy when I asked her how she felt about knowing she would be crossing over soon. "Andy, I declare to you that I have never, ever in my whole life had the absolute sense of deep peace in my heart that I have right now." I knew she was telling me like it was because of the timbre and tone of her voice. I pray to be like Jane when my days are up and it is time to go Home. I pray to keep the faith like she did.

FIGHT TO LIVE WITH ALL YOUR MIGHT . . .

Paul sums up his expectations to young Timothy: "Now there is in store for me the crown of righteousness, which the Lord, the righteous Judge, will award to me on that day—and not only to me, but also to all who have longed for his appearing" (2 Timothy 4:8). According to tradition, within months of writing this letter sometime during AD 65, Paul was led out from the Mamertine Prison to the third milestone marker on the Ostian Road in Rome, and beheaded. The exact place of his execution is said to be Aquae Salviae, and on that location today stands a basilica called St. Paul Outside the Walls. Paul's fight was fought, his race finished. He kept the faith. And Jesus Himself welcomed him home. Someday He will welcome you and me, too.

Fear says, "if only." Faith declares, "nevertheless." What words are you speaking these days? I can't help but think how much more God would have been pleased with me as a father all those years ago if, even

☼

A MARATHON RUNNER ONCE GAVE THE SECRET OF HIS ENDURANCE:

"As I stand at the starting line, I know that somewhere out there is a finish line." Out there somewhere is a finish line for all of us. So fight the good fight, not if only, but nevertheless. Finish your race, not if only, but nevertheless. Keep the faith, not if only, but nevertheless. In other words, live with all your might now, while you do live.

when my kids were small and we were up to our necks in "if-onlys," I had trusted Him enough to revel in the little joys of the "nevertheless." I mostly anchored my soul in those days to the fear that God's grace would prove insufficient for the grinding challenges we felt we faced. So I procrastinated in pursuing the fullness of joy until the conditions I foolishly thought were essential to joy were realized. How shortsighted. As a result, how much did I miss? How much richer could those precious years with my little ones have been? Would not showing faith that honors God have produced, by His grace, even more such joyous moments, only deeper still? I do not know.

But this I have learned: the fullness of life that God has for us comes, not in the "if-only," but in the "nevertheless." Especially here in the Valley, I can't afford to blow it like that again, and so as your Travel Writer I am determined never again to squander a good "nevertheless" in my life (and neither should you). Remember Jesus' words, "Your business is life, not death. And life is urgent . . ."

It's a good way to roll. I commend it to you all.

Your "Anything but Wait"
Travel Writer,

Pastor Andy

AFTER-THOUGHTS: HINNAINEE

THE PERSON WHOM GOD CALLED SIMPLY REPLIED WITH THE HEBREW WORD HINNAINEE (HIN-NAY'-NEE), THE WORD OF THE SERVANT—WHICH MEANS "HERE I AM"—AVAILABLE—READY TO SERVE—"WHAT MAY I DO FOR YOU?"[1]

My Dear Fellow Travelers,

By now you have been in the Valley long enough to get the lay of the land. I trust that my little notes have been of service in helping you to adjust to your journey. I hope you will presently find yourself in a position to tender advice to those who now come behind you to this place. That is, I believe, how it should be. Advance scouts in distant lands sending back reports of what wonders and terrors the new place presents, and how to navigate them. I pray that I have done a passable job of that for you. Now, my friends, we go forward, doing it together and with our heavenly Father.

A couple of months into my adventure in Cancerland, I sat with an old friend who has been a Christian leader for over thirty years. He knew I had been through surgery, was being tortured with chemotherapy, and was facing a real chance of dying soon. And he asked me, "Andy, is God as big for you now as He was before all this happened?"

Instantly I knew what lurked behind that question. All the years that the both of us had stood in hospital rooms and with funeral biers and by deathbeds reciting hopeful words of Scripture and intoning the bold words "behold, I show you a mystery." Was all of that true? Really? When push comes to shove and it is the preacher in the batter's box and not just in the press box, in the hospital bed and not just standing next to it with a Bible, how do all of those words go down? Poignantly and with brave honesty, my pastor friend was seeking confirmation of the faith he had preached to thousands for years, as had I. He just wanted to know with certainty what he and I had been promoting in faith: have we been pointing people in the right direction after all?

All I could do was smile and say, "Hey my friend, He's bigger . . . way bigger than we even thought." I believe that one of the main purposes of God in taking me through this trial was so that I would find Him stronger than ever in it. So that I could sense His presence, not in spite of my suffering, but because of it. So that I would know for a fact that underneath me *are* His everlasting arms, that His banner over me *is* love, that His Holy Spirit *is* ever present with me, and that Christ's strength was constantly and powerfully on display even in my distress. So that I would know with certainty that, when the going does get rough and more than sugary words and spiritual bromides are required, the gospel truly does hold fast after all.

When I answered my friend with those words, a noticeable wave of relief moved across his features. "I am so glad to hear that." He was not only relieved to know that, as a pastor, he was indeed telling people the truth when he shared God's promises. He was relieved to know that, when his own turn in the batter's box (of facing his own mortality) came around, the very words of comfort he had spoken to thousands would prove true for himself as well. He knew that one of the greatest tasks we living ones face is approaching our inevitable death with faith, hope, and love and that entering the Valley flips the on switch to that challenge. He was just glad to have confirmed what he had always believed, that yes, God is big enough to see us through, all the way through, even this Valley of the Shadow of Death.

FURTHER UP, FURTHER IN

Paradoxically, I have written to you that this strange land of shadows is a place of peace. It is so because the Great Shepherd is there leading His sheep who trust Him no matter what, even as they approach their journey's destination. So we resonate with the sweet singer of Israel, David, as he writes, "Yea, though I walk through the valley of the shadow of death, I will fear no evil: for thou art with me; thy rod and thy staff they comfort me" (Psalm 23:4 KJV). Neither did the great Puritan John Bunyan fear in the Valley. His writings in *Pilgrim's Progress* prove that he knew the Valley was not a destination but a passageway: "Now at the end of this valley was another, called the Valley of the Shadow of Death; and Christian must go through it, because the way to the Celestial City lay through the midst of it." The ultimate progress of God's pilgrims is heaven, and all who have faith in Christ gladly traverse the Valley to arrive there.

We pilgrims in this Valley know that death is like a shadow that surrounds us constantly. But we need not fear, for we know that a mere shadow cannot ultimately hurt us. Our faith teaches us that death itself has been defeated by Christ and that we are privileged to walk in that victory. We fear no shadows and no evil in the Valley because our Great Shepherd's presence guides us and His rod and staff comfort us on the way.

Is God big enough to see us all the way through the Valley of the Shadow of Death? Oh yes He is, and that is the first and most important fact to be learned upon coming to this place. We all have to die of something, someday. If indeed it will be the cancer that brought us to the Valley, so be it. If cancer is the rod and staff of My Shepherd leading me to the Celestial City, then I call it my Moses for guiding me out of the bondage of making bricks in this world and for moving me from the old to the new.

> *The difference between the old Narnia and the new Narnia was like that. The new one was a deeper country: every rock and flower and blade of grass looked like it meant more. . . . It was the unicorn who summed up what everyone was feeling. He stamped his right fore-hoof*

on the ground and neighed, and then cried: "I have come home at last! This is my real country! I belong here. This is the land I have been looking for all my life, though I never knew it till now. The reason why we loved the old Narnia so much is because it sometimes looked a little like this. Come further up, come further in!"[2]

HINNAINEE

It is not only the privilege of the children of God to come further up and further in. It is their destiny. Whether it is cancer that moves us "further" or mere old age or any other cause of death by which humans shuffle off their mortal coil, the result is the same. We cross over. We realize our eternal destiny. We complete the journey home. All of us do this. All of us *must* do this. The question is not "if," but when. Here in the Valley, the assumption is that the "when" is sooner rather than later. But still we do not know for certain. How could we? God may heal us of this disease and send us back to serve Him in Myopia. Or He may keep us in the Valley far longer than we imagined because He has a purpose for us to serve in this place.

This we do know: God tells no one any story but his own. And since He is the Great Storyteller and not us, we have to factor the divine serendipity into our trek through this Valley. We may die soon, and preparation for that possible eventuality is essential. But so also is preparation for staying alive for a long time to come. In short, our posture as travelers in the Valley must be the same as our posture as Christ-following travelers in Myopia—the posture of a disciple.

Disciples serve their Master no matter what. They serve when times are good, and they serve when times are tough. They serve on the mountaintop. And yes, they serve here in the Valley too. They understand that the true test of discipleship is service under pressure. And so they stand ready, in season and out, to hear and respond to their Master's voice. Just consider the following: "God called to Abraham saying, 'Abraham' and he replied, "Here I am, Lord'" (Genesis 22:1).

☼

"If we answer the call to discipleship, where will it lead us? What decisions and partings will it demand? To answer this question we shall have to go to Him, for only He knows the answer. Only Jesus Christ who bids us follow Him, knows the journey's end. But we do know that it will be a road of boundless mercy. Discipleship means joy."[3]

An angel spoke to Jacob in a dream and he replied, "Here I am, Lord" (Genesis 31:11). From a burning bush God called "Moses" and he replied, "Here I am, Lord" (Exodus 3:4). God asked Isaiah, "Whom shall I send?" he replied, "Here am I, send me!" (Isaiah 6:8). After the angel Gabriel told Mary she would bear Jesus, the son of God, she replied, "Here I am, the servant of the Lord; let it be with me according to your word" (Luke 1:38). Of these instances and others like them, E. Stanley Ott offers the following insight: "In every case, the person whom God called simply replied with the Hebrew word hinnainee (hin-nay'-nee), the word of the servant—which means "here I am"—available—ready to serve—"what may I do for you?"

God is always calling His people to serve. Sometimes the context for that service is loving others in His name, or sharing the good news of the gospel, or obeying Him when it would be a large sight easier to bug out and do it our own way. Other times the context for that service is simply remaining faithful during times of pain, or suffering, or disappointment. The key for us is not the context of our call, but the answer we give to the One who issues it. We can either say, "Not now Lord, could You please just pick on someone else," or "hinnainee." As your Travel Writer, I do recommend the latter response. As a Valley dweller now, you will find that it promotes a far more joyful, meaningful, and productive journey.

EVEN THOSE WHO SEEM SECURE

But wait. Is not committing myself to serve Christ even in this Valley a futile gesture? After all, it takes time to serve and time is not exactly an abundant commodity in this place, or at least it does not appear to be. That is a common, if mistaken, objection, based on the false notion that time is abundant in Myopia. See how King David dispels that idea in Psalm 39:4–5: "Show me, Lord, my life's end and the number of my days; let me know how fleeting my life is. You have made my days a mere handbreadth; the span of my years is as nothing before you. Everyone is but a breath, even those who seem secure."

As a Valley dweller, I get a wry smile on my face when I read that last phrase, "even those who seem secure." Perhaps you do too, and for the same reason as me: we all *used* to be there. It took our trip to the Valley to show us how fleeting our lives truly are, even our lives in Myopia.

And so allow me to expose a not-so-hidden secret: we are all in the Valley, not just those who suffer with cancer. Everybody—healthy and young as well as sick and old—we are *all* in the Valley because life is fleeting. Not to put too morbid a spin on it, but it is at the moment of each human birth that the countdown clock to death begins ticking. Therefore Myopia is also the land of the dying, not just the Valley.

True, when you come to this land of the shadow, you are probably closer to the celestial gateway and so you behold a different scenery in the shade cast by encroaching Valley walls. It does seem like a new land. It does feel like a different country. But it really is not. The whole world is the land of the dying. The Valley is just a subset of that world in which the ultimate destination of all of our journeys is more closely at hand. So realistically, all of us this side of heaven are traversing the Valley of mortality and every travel tip your humble Travel Writer has offered is not just for cancer patients, but for people everywhere. "Everyone is but a breath . . . *even those who seem secure*" (italics mine).

ALL THE TIME THERE IS

So let us all be intent upon experiencing the precious moments of our lives to the full, not just in the Valley, but in Myopia as well. Let us make the most of the story God is telling in each of our lives without dissembling and without delay. For if we do, we will not lack the time required to accomplish what God has for each of us to do. Before he crossed over to heaven, our fellow Valley dweller Dr. Richard John Neuhaus discovered this truth. "Having never stopped to live the present moment, we one day run out of present moments and discover we have not lived at all. It is true in every present moment: you have all the time there is."[4]

You have all the time there is to trust God as He spins a beautiful story of faith, hope, and love in your life. You have all the time there is to experience the powerful and ineffable presence of Immanuel every moment of your journey. You have all the time there is to exercise your faith by praying prayers to your heavenly Father that are persistent, patient, and pliable. You have all the time there is to trust the goodness of God even in your pain so your suffering drops like stars. You have all the time there is to engage the process of crossing over to heaven with peace and great anticipation. You have all the time there is to traverse even this Valley of the Shadow with hope that does not fail or fade away. You have all the time there is to progress in all the things that matter most—what you believe and who you are and what you do. You have all the time there is for the most precious thing—loving and being loved. You have all the time there is to wait on the Lord, staying in the freefall with unshakeable confidence that He has you in the palm of His hands. You have all the time there is to live fully, to live well, and to live with every last ounce of love and energy and opportunity that God gives you. Let not your heart be troubled. While still in this Valley, you have all the time there is.

CARPE AETERNITATEM

So do I. As my friend Scott McClellan wrote about me, I have all the time there is and that gives me hope.

> *What we hope for should always be second to what—or who—we hope in. Andy hoped he would beat the cancer and spend a couple more decades here on Earth. He made no bones about that. But the source of his calm was a short phrase in the middle of a passage he quoted from Psalm 39: "My hope is in you." . . . Andy did beat that cancer, by the way. Four years later, he's still easygoing, and he's still riding that Harley. Our community praised God when the chemo worked and the scans came back clean, but not because God had demonstrated Himself worthy of our affection by healing our pastor. No, we praised God because we had expe-*

rienced a little bit of what it meant to place our hope in Him whether sick or well. As Christians we may or may not receive what we hope for, but the One we hope in stands ready to give of Himself instead."[5]

I am grateful for this respite called "remission," though I am not fooled by it. My oncologist gently insists that I not consider myself cured until at least ten years clear of cancer have passed. That means I am still both-feet-planted here in the Valley for at least seven more years . . . and the journey continues. But that is just fine with me. After what I have experienced here, I know that even if I make it back to Myopia, there will always be the awareness that, with the whole human race, I am still in the Valley—just perhaps not the very shadowy part.

This realization has afforded me new motivation as your Travel Writer to move past the *carpe diem* to *carpe aeternitatem*: "seize eternity." In the words of my friend Rob Quiring,

> *If our vision is focused on the moment only, if we live only for the day, if the value of our lives is predicated on becoming fertilizer for flowers, then we are not truly living life from the perspective we should as Christians. As Christians we live not only in the here and now, but we will live on into eternity and so Carpe Aeternitatem—seize eternity. Why settle for just a day? Eternity matters. To live well as a Christian, you must live each day in the light of eternity.*

So, by the grace of God and with you my fellow travelers, I will do. And though we know He tells no one any story but their own, I suspect He will allow us all to celebrate the winsome tale He is spinning in all of our lives as we follow our Great Shepherd through this Valley of the Shadow.

Hinnainee,

Pastor Andy

NOTES

WELCOME: TRAVEL TIPS FOR THE VALLEY

1. Walter Wangerin's *Letters from the Land of Cancer* is the inspiration for this appellation.
2. Perceptibly written in an email to me about who is the true audience for this very book.
3. Well, perhaps minus the supplications for Guinness . . . unless you are an Irishman like me with an appreciation for God's good gifts of black lager and fine stogies.
4. In an email from my friend Dr. Larry Parsley that challenged me to share my sojourn in the Valley with others who follow behind me into this place.

1: STORY—GOD TELLS YOURS

1. C. S. Lewis, *The Horse and His Boy* (New York: Harper Collins, 2005), 140–42.
2. Christopher Hitchens, "Topic of Cancer," *Vanity Fair,* September 2010.
3. 1 Corinthians 6:3.
4. The writer to the Hebrews affirmed this victory: "Since the children have flesh and blood, he too shared in their humanity so that by his death he might break the power of him who holds the power of death—that is, the devil—and free those who all their lives were held in slavery by their fear of death" (Hebrews 2:14–15). Our faith is in the ultimate victory of Christ and in our eternal life with Him in heaven.
5. Tim Keller, *King's Cross* (New York: Dutton Redeemer, 2011), 16–17.
6. John Calvin, *Institutes of Christian Religion* (vol 1, ch 18), 203 [referencing Augustine, *Expositions on the Book of Psalms,* Ps 11:2].

2: IMMANUEL—GOD IS WITH YOU

1. Donner Atwood, *Reformed Review,* qtd. in *Leadership 4,* no. 4 (1983): 87.
2. "Where Everybody Knows Your Name": theme from the Paramount Television series *Cheers* by Gary Portnoy and Judy Hart (Angelo) (Paramount Television Productions; Addax Music Company, Inc.; 1982).

3. Verla Gillmor, "What to do when life is dark and heaven's quiet." http://www.fibrotalk.com/forum/viewtopic.php?f=34&t=8061.
4. William J. Stuntz, "Three Gifts for Hard Times," *CT Classic,* August 28, 2009. http://www.christianitytoday.com/ct/2009/august/34.44.html.
5. Ibid.
6. Randy Alcorn, *If God Is Good: Faith in the Midst of Suffering and Evil* (Colorado Springs: Multnomah, 2009), 399.
7. Quote attributed to St. Francis de Sales, 1567–1622.

3: BELIEVE—PRAY ACCORDINGLY

1. Warren Wiersbe, *The Wycliffe Handbook of Preaching and Preachers* (Chicago: Moody, 1984), 242.
2. John Ortberg, *God Is Closer Than You Think* (Grand Rapids: Zondervan, 2005), 24–25.
3. 1 Thessalonians 4:13–18.
4. Romans 8:23.
5. These adverbs are drawn from the concluding section of Dr. Ray Pritchard's excellent sermon on prayer from James 5 (www.keepbelieving.com/sermon/praying-for-the-sick).
6. James 5:16.

4: STARS—THE BEAUTY OF SUFFERING

1. Rob Bell, *Drops Like Stars* (Grand Rapids: Zondervan: 2009), 130.
2. I'm confident that this is not "TMI," too much information, for fellow Valley travelers. In fact, it's probably not information at all to them, but rather experience.
3. David M. Augenstein, "Wholesome Words: Accurately Speaking and Teaching the Word of Truth." http://biblebreath.wordpress.com/2009/06/13/accurately-speaking-and-teaching-the-word-of-truth/.
4. *The Gulag Archipelago: 1918–1956, vol 2,* part IV, "The Soul and Barbed Wire" (New York: Harper Perennial Modern Classics, 2002).
5. Rob Bell, *Drops Like Stars,* 124.
6. This is the Protestant take on the ministry value of suffering. Note that it is not quite as developed as the Catholic view as expressed by

Jeffry Hendrix: "So the Catholic church says, this is your opportunity. Use your suffering, your grief, even your demise for the good of those who need it. This is the work of redemptive suffering, and it is called 'offering it up.' Archbishop Fulton Sheen once said that when we 'assist' at Mass—when we participate in the Holy Sacrifice of the Mass—our suffering, our aloneness, our death, all the things we are going through are united with His Crucifixion and Resurrection in a state of grace that we receive by faith. And if that wasn't enough, Saint Paul reverses the flow, so to speak, and says that our suffering, our anguish, peril, and, yes, our death completes the redemptive work of Our Lord (Col 1.23b-24). By being willing to unite our suffering to His in this way we win even more grace" (Jeffry Hendrix, *A Little Guide for Your Last Days* (Plano, TX: Bridegroom Press, 2009), 79.

7. Thomas Lynch, *The Undertaking* (New York: W. W. Norton, 1997), 97–98.
8. William Stuntz, *CT Classic*, "Three Gifts for Hard Times," August 2009.

5: HOMECOMING—THE GOODNESS OF GOD

1. William Law, *Christian Perfection* (Carol Stream, IL: Creation House, 1975).
2. Julie Rhodes, www.mom2momdfw.com. June 2009.
3. James Van Tholen, "Surprised by Death," *Christianity Today*, May 24, 1999.
4. Richard John Neuhaus, *As I Lay Dying* (New York: Basic Books, 2002), 3.
5. Tony Snow, "Cancer's Unexpected Blessings" *CT*, July 20, 2007.
6. Mitch Albom, *Tuesdays with Morrie* (New York: Broadway Books, 2007), 82.
7. Walter Wangerin, *Letters from the Land of Cancer* (Grand Rapids: Zondervan: 2010), 43.
8. Thomas Lynch, *The Undertaking* (New York: W. W. Norton, 1997), 81.
9. C. S. Lewis, *The Last Battle* (New York: Harper Collins, 1956), 228.

6: HOPE—TOO ACCUSTOMED TO DARKNESS

1. Scott McClellan, "How We Misunderstand Hope," *Relevant Magazine*, June 6, 2013.
2. Barbara Ehrenreich, *Bright-Sided: How the Relentless Promotion of Positive Thinking Has Undermined America* (New York: Metropolitan Books, 2009), 44.
3. Scott McClellan, "How We Misunderstand Hope."

4. Frederick Buechner, *The Longing for Home* (San Francisco: Harper San Francisco, 1996), 148.

5. Barbara Taylor, "Can These Bones Live?" *Christian Century*, vol 113, no 9, March 13 (1996).

6. Frederick Buechner, *The Longing for Home*, 149.

7. Randy Alcorn, *If God Is Good* (Colorado Springs, CO: Multnomah Books, 2009), 14.

8. Scott McClellan, "How We Misunderstand Hope."

7: TREASURE—THE THINGS THAT MATTER MOST

1. Joyce M. Schutt, "Consumer's Prayer" in Ann Landers' column, Feb 2, 1998.

2. Ron Underwood, *City Slickers* (Columbia Pictures, 1991).

3. William H. Smith, "On Being Average," *World Magazine*, vol 13, no 19, May 16, 1998. www.worldmag.com/1998/05/on_being_average.

4. C. S. Lewis, *Mere Christianity* (New York: Harper Collins, 1952), 50.

5. John Eldridge, *Waking the Dead* (Nashville: Thomas Nelson, 2003), 56.

6. R. Kent Hughes, *Philippians, Colossians, and Philemon: The Fellowship of the Gospel and the Supremacy of Christ, Preaching the Word* (Wheaton, Illinois: Crossway, 2013).

8: LOVE—THE MOST PRECIOUS THING

1. Brennan Manning, *The Ragamuffin Gospel* (Sisters, OR: Multnomah Publishers, 2000), 88.

2. www.sounddude.com/sounddude_files/bloom2.htm.

3. Tony Snow, "Cancer's Unexpected Blessings," *Christianity Today*, July 20, 2007.

4. C. S. Lewis, *The Four Loves* (New York: Harcourt Brace, 1960), 122.

5. www.frederickbuechner.com/content/inspection-sticker.

9: WAIT—STAY IN THE FREEFALL

1. Bill Hybels, *Too Busy Not to Pray* (Downers Grove, IL: IVP Books, 2008), 93.

2. Frank Darabont, *Shawshank Redemption* (PolyGram Film International, 1994).

3. James Packer, *In God's Presence* (Wheaton, IL: H. Shaw Publishers, 2000), 20.

4. "Good Friday: When There's Rescue and There's Not" by Rebekah Lyons, http://www.qideas.org/articles/.

10: LIVE—ALL THE TIME THERE IS

1. Tony Snow, "Cancer's Unexpected Blessings," *Christianity Today*, July 20, 2007.

2. Jason Lehman poem (Dear Abby).

3. Clarence Jordan, *Cotton Patch Gospel: Paul's Epistles* (Macon, GA: Smyth & Helwys, 2004), 75.

4. *Discipleship Journal*, issue 42, 1987.

AFTERTHOUGHTS: HINNAINEE

1. E. Stanley Ott, "Here I Am," Building One Another E-Letter, vol 8, no 27 (part 1), July 20, 2009.

2. C. S. Lewis, *The Last Battle* (New York: Harper Collins, 2005), 212–13.

3. Dietrich Bonhoeffer, *The Cost of Discipleship* (New York: Touchstone, 1995), 32.

4. Richard John Neuhaus, *As I Lay Dying* (New York: Basic Books, 2002), 66.

5. Scott McClellan, "How We Misunderstand Hope," *Relevant Magazine*, June 6, 2013.

I commend my heartfelt gratitude to

. . . Alice, my wife and also now for thirty-six years my best friend, for bearing the brunt of my cancer battle with a courageous faith and good cheer that still grips my heart even as I type these words. She is my hero, as are my children . . . Julie (and son-in-law Gordon), Elizabeth, Bonnie, Jonathan, and Jeffrey . . . each of whom was a greater rock of faith and hope and help to their dad than they'll ever know.

. . . Dr. Richard Johnston, Dr. Steven Wilkofsky, Dr. Randy Crim, Dr. Gerald Edelman, and Dr. Edward Clifford, my mighty quintet of medical masters who, in the hands of God, diagnosed, dissected, and injected me from Stage IV colon cancer into complete remission in just over two years' time.

. . . the wonderful nurses at Irving Baylor Hospital and Texas Oncology who had a knack for making me love them even though it regularly felt like they were trying to kill me ("wounds of a friend"!). I've heard of the Stockholm Syndrome, but this is ridiculous! No really, my Alice is a nurse and so I know and appreciate now more than ever who truly does the heavy lifting in patient care.

. . . David Dendy who at the outset of my chemo told me that every man needs someone to love, something to do, and something to look forward to, then proceeded to organize a post-cancer cross-country motorcycle trip (what faith!) with a bunch of my biker friends who also pitched in to buy me a one-of-a-kind Harley (Street Glide CVO, if you must know) for the trip they just organized. That was a far more enjoyable journey than my previous trek through the Valley . . . thanks, my biker bros!

. . . Allen Arnold, Ray Pritchard, Matt Chandler, and Philip Rawley who, as my pastor/writer friends advised, helped, cajoled, and motivated me in getting this book out of my heart and onto the hard drive.

. . . Donna O'Reilly, intrepid executive assistant without whose cheerful assistance I'm quite sure not one deadline would have been hit.

. . . My "Bent Tree Boys" Pastors' group (Gary Brandenburg, Steve Hixon, Chris Freeland, Larry Parsley, Dale Patterson, Steve Stroope, Pete Briscoe, Jeff Jones, Bruce Miller, Toby Slough, Chip Bell, Jeff Warren) whose shoulder-to-shoulder circle of ministry support for fifteen years only strengthened when cancer hit.

. . . Duane Sherman and Pam Pugh, Moody editors extraordinaire who discovered the words of yet one more authorial newbie and made them better for this book.

. . . and Mike Trabun who edited the manuscript to NOTES as a prelude to embarking on his own foray into the Valley. May your journey, my friend, be blessed as you made mine to be . . .

Eric Andrew McQuitty

More from Moody Publishers . . .

Do you ever wonder about heaven? Heaven should be something to look forward to, not something to be confused about. Follow along as Dr. Enns succinctly and personally leads you through what the Bible has to say about heaven. We all need hope—hope for our loved ones who are now gone and hope for ourselves as eternity draws closer.

From the Word to Life

From the Word ***to Life***

Moody Radio produces and delivers compelling programs filled with biblical insights and creative expressions of faith that help you take the next step in your relationship with Christ.

You can hear Moody Radio on 36 stations and more than 1,500 radio outlets across the U.S. and Canada. Or listen on your smartphone with the Moody Radio app!

www.moodyradio.org